FAILING AMERICA'S FAITHFUL

FAILING AMERICA'S FAITHFUL

How Today's Churches
Are Mixing God with
Politics and Losing
Their Way

KATHLEEN KENNEDY TOWNSEND

WARNER BOOKS

NEW YORK   BOSTON

Warner Books

Hachette Book Group USA
1271 Avenue of the Americas
New York, NY 10020
Visit our Web site at www.HachetteBookGroupUSA.com.

Printed in the United States of America

First Edition: March 2007
10 9 8 7 6 5 4 3 2 1

Library of Congress Cataloging-in-Publication Data
Townsend, Kathleen.
    Failing America's faithful : how today's churches are mixing God with
politics and losing their way / Kathleen Kennedy Townsend. — 1st ed.
        p. cm.
    Includes bibliographical references.
    ISBN-13: 978-0-446-57715-1
    ISBN-10: 0-446-57715-4
    1. Christianity and politics—United States. 2. Christian sociology—United
States. I. Title.
    BR526.T72 2007
    261.70973—dc22   2006007523

Book design by Charles Sutherland

To David, with so much love and thanks, and for Meaghan, Maeve, Kate, and Kerry, whose vitality and passion give me great hope for the future.

ACKNOWLEDGMENTS

———— ∞ ————

F riends both old and new took time from their busy schedules to talk about the challenge of creating a progressive Church. Father Robert Drinan, a model of spiritual and political leadership, former member of Congress, and the priest who baptized our fourth daughter, has been generous with his time, his wisdom, and ideas of people with whom I should speak. The same is true of Fathers Joseph Boyle and William Meninger from the St. Benedict's Monastery, a Trappist community in Colorado, who have been enormously thoughtful in their discussion of forgiveness, the challenge of evil, and the future of the Church.

One of the great pleasures of the last few years has been discussing the Catholic Church with extraordinary nuns. More than ever, I believe they are the Church's most persuasive and inspiring representatives. I am particularly indebted to Pat Smith, Charlotte Kerr, Joan Chittister, Anne Curtis, Catherine Pinkerton, Maria McCoy, Sharon Euart, Mary Johnson, Mary Aquin O'Neill, Diana Caplin, Sandra Schneiders, Janet Eisner, and Maureen Fielder.

I'm grateful also to Catholic University president David O'Connell for putting me in touch with some brilliant scholars from his institution. Sister Rita Larivee, Father Charlie Curran, and Theresa Kane, from the *National Catholic Reporter*, on whose board I sit, are inspirations. Their courage and vision are constant sources of inspiration.

I continue to believe that the lay leadership will serve as the source for a revitalization of the Catholic Church. I was fortunate to be able to draw on many of their experiences and perspectives. I am especially grateful to John DiIulio, Governor Kathleen Sebelius, Jim Slattery, and Geoffrey Boisi.

Peter Barnes and Jonathan Rowe facilitated my stay at the Mesa Writers Refuge. The Kennedy School of Government invited me as a visiting fellow, giving me the chance to spend time with Father Bryan Hehir, former dean of the Harvard Divinity School, who was unstintingly generous with his learning.

The richness of the history of Protestant progressivism was one of the most gratifying discoveries of my writing. I had many guides, and wish to thank the Reverend Frank Reed of Bethel AME Church in Baltimore, Rev. Kerry Hill, Forrest Church, Rev. Richard Mau, Jimmy Creech, Ronald Sider, Tony Campolo, Rev. Bob Edgar, Susan Thistlewaite, Welton Gaddy, Martin Marty, James Dunn, David Beckmann, Richard Parker, Cathy Isaacson, Allan and Susan Tibbels, Rick and Kay Warren, and Jim Wallis.

I never would have been able to write this book without the encouragement and wise counsel of so many friends. Many thanks to Alan and Dafna Fleischmann, Janet and Jeff Hanson, Tommy Caplan, Howard Friedman, Daphna Ziman, Michael Sarbanes, Vinny DeMarco, Marie Day, Marvin Masterson, Dave Hornbeck, Heidi Hartmann, John Brophy, and Willie and Finley Lewis. Terry Lierman, as far as I'm concerned, defines what it means to be a good neighbor. Stacie Rivera has been with me since my 1994 campaign. Her friendship and faith have been indispensable to me in more ways than I could ever count.

As a first-time author, I was fortunate to have so many friends and colleagues to mentor me through this process. Charlie Peters, who first published my articles on religion and politics more than two decades ago in *The Washington Monthly*, was wonderfully supportive, as were Phil Keisling, Steve Waldman, and Jonathan Rowe.

The final shape of the book owes much to the insightful work of Danny Franklin. Others who have been supportive in a variety of ways include Sarah Blustain, Afsaneh Beschloss, Judy Feder, Linc Caplan, Jim Kennedy, Josh Greenman, and Phil Noble.

My agent, Mel Berger, has offered patient and even-tempered advice. Diana Baroni and Les Pockell at Warner Books have been charitable and gentle with their editorial advice.

I would never have attempted to write such a book without my husband, David. He is a brilliant teacher and was unfailingly patient and kind as he discussed my ideas and suggested books I should examine. Finally, we are blessed with four glorious daughters, Meaghan, Maeve, Kate, and Kerry, who were curious, excited, and challenging about this book and so much more.

CONTENTS

CHAPTER ONE: A Spiritual Awakening 1

CHAPTER TWO: Much Is Expected 32

CHAPTER THREE: God's Work Must Truly Be Our Own: The Catholic Church's Tradition of Social Justice 65

CHAPTER FOUR: The Progressive Protestant Tradition 88

CHAPTER FIVE: What Does It Mean to Be a Christian Nation? 109

CHAPTER SIX: Misbegotten Males and Other Misconceptions: Where the Catholic Church Went Wrong 128

CHAPTER SEVEN: Moses Didn't Have a Bake Sale 152

CHAPTER EIGHT: Write the Vision on the Tablets 174

BIBLIOGRAPHY 199

FAILING
AMERICA'S
FAITHFUL

The Parable of the Good Samaritan

And, behold, a certain lawyer stood up, and tempted him, saying, Master, what shall I do to inherit eternal life?

He said unto him, What is written in the law? how readest thou?

And he answering said, Thou shalt love the Lord thy God with all thy heart, and with all thy soul, and with all thy strength, and with all thy mind; and thy neighbour as thyself.

And he said unto him, Thou hast answered right: this do, and thou shalt live.

But he, willing to justify himself, said unto Jesus, And who is my neighbour?

And Jesus answering said, A certain man went down from Jerusalem to Jericho, and fell among thieves, which stripped him of his raiment, and wounded him, and departed, leaving him half dead.

And by chance there came down a certain priest that way: and when he saw him, he passed by on the other side.

And likewise a Levite, when he was at the place, came and looked on him, and passed by on the other side.

But a certain Samaritan, as he journeyed, came where he was: and when he saw him, he had compassion on him,

And went to him, and bound up his wounds, pouring in oil and wine, and set him on his own beast, and brought him to an inn, and took care of him.

And on the morrow when he departed, he took out two pence, and gave them to the host, and said unto him, Take care of him; and whatsoever thou spendest more, when I come again, I will repay thee.

Which now of these three, thinkest thou, was neighbour unto him that fell among the thieves?

And he said, He that shewed mercy on him. Then said Jesus unto him, Go, and do thou likewise.

LUKE 10:25–37 (KING JAMES VERSION)

CHAPTER ONE

A Spiritual Awakening

―❮❮❮❯❯❯―

Now, more than ever before, we Americans are finding faith. We are improving our lives—learning through faith to be kind to ourselves, to our spouses and children, to our neighbors. We are giving charity through our churches. We are speaking about morality and values in a way we haven't done in a generation. If the great anxiety of moral folks since the 1960s was that America was in danger of becoming a country of empty values—an amusement park illuminated by self-interest, consumerism, and Hollywood-inspired ambition—they should no longer fear. *The Passion of the Christ* was one of the most popular films of 2004. Twenty-two percent of Americans said "moral values" was the most important issue for them in the 2004 presidential election—yes, a minority, but a huge number when you consider that we were also a country at war in a failing economy. This is not the 1990s decade of stock market bubbles and rampant materialism. This is the decade of faith.

And yet I wonder. In my lifetime, even while faith has expanded its reach, it has become narrower. When I was a child, we learned that to be religious was to be part of a community, and that the purpose of our faith was to improve the world, not just our own lives. In this theology, the individual prayer was a droplet in a global lake, rippling its effects out to the farthest edges of the pool. I was a teenager and young adult in the turbulent years of the 1960s and 1970s, when America was riven by cultural change. This turbulence touched my family daily. How did we respond? In our Catholic church and in our home we prayed to be good and virtuous. We prayed for my uncle John Kennedy, and my father, Robert Kennedy, to be the best public servants that they could be. We prayed that our leaders would have the strength to go forth and help those starving children in Mississippi or West Virginia. (And yes, there are children in America whose lives are just as desperate today as they were when my father toured the country and told us, his blue eyes dark with outrage and his hands shaking, what he had found, hidden, in this great country.) And finally, we prayed that our government would have the good sense and good grace to put into place policies that would help not only us but also every person in America to live with dignity.

Today, that is not what I see. Don't get me wrong: You may pray and give money to your church, and give support through your church to all sorts of good causes, as do I. But fear and intolerance have taken hold. Instead of emphasizing the fact that we are all children of God, faith in America now divides communities. Virtue is something that takes place in your own home, in your church, and perhaps in your neighborhood if you are very lucky. The fastest-growing churches in the country—evangelical churches—tend to emphasize personal salvation over the creation of a more just nation. And many of those churches, along with my own Catholic Church, are using "moral values" as a code with which to attack those who don't believe as we do. Most of the millions of dollars congregants give to churches every year go not to help the needy outside of the church community, but for infrastructure and expansion of their own churches. Our priests and ministers send us out into the world to find others whose faith most resembles our own, not to work every day for those who need us most, regardless of their faith. Today faith builds walls to keep the threatening, encroaching world out, rather than moving us in ever-widening ways into the world that so desperately needs our help.

And our culture supports this inward turn. In the 1990s I was the lieutenant governor of Maryland, where I tried to make my drop of prayer ripple out. I spent my days pushing—pushing government officials, community leaders, businesspeople, schoolchildren—to support initiatives that promoted justice to the widest possible community: fighting drug use, reducing gun violence, putting into place character education, providing health care to children, protecting the Chesapeake Bay. These programs worked. When I ran for governor in 2002, the *Washington Post* praised me as a politician with a "moral compass." Nonetheless, I saw that these values did not turn people on. As I campaigned across the state, voters would shake my hand and then, as soon as I began to tell them what we had achieved and what needed to be done, I could see their eyes glaze over; they were simply not as excited about these results as I was.

I'm still asking myself, Why? Why did a majority not feel, personally, the suffering and the need of their neighbors and the commitment to make communities stronger? I don't have all the answers, but I know that we have gotten out of the habit of thinking of ourselves as part of the wider world. We no longer hear in our churches, or in our homes, the daily reminder that to walk in God's path is not just to pray or give charity, but also to work for *justice* for every creature on His earth.

This book is a reveille in which I hope to share the spiritual awakening that shaped my life and I hope will enlighten yours—giving us the courage to renew our country's great promise.

To some, spiritual awakenings come in a sudden

flash of recognition and revelation. But my spiritual awakening, as I suspect is true for many others', has steadily unfolded over the course of my life as I gained a deeper understanding of the truths I learned as a youth. I knew as a young girl that God created me, loved me, and wanted what was best for me as He did all his creatures. With the passing of years, and the tragedies and challenges that I have had to face, I have had to struggle to reclaim my faith, and the strength to fight for justice that goes hand in hand with it. Many times I have had to find hope even in terrible loss, and I have had to learn to immerse myself in life's challenges rather than to run away in fear. But these tests have only deepened my understanding of the power of God's love and the obligations that come along with it. Now, I'm struck with how it has given me the ability to look at the world with new eyes and see how truly blessed I and, indeed, all humanity is. I have seen how good the world can be and the responsibility we share to make it better for everyone.

Not so long ago, our churches helped engage their congregations in the fight for social justice in the world. But today I am unhappy and dissatisfied with my Church and its failure to honor its best traditions. It is time for all of us to do what we can to reclaim those traditions, and to reclaim our churches.

When I was twelve years old, I lost my uncle John Kennedy, who was one of America's most beloved presidents, in a brutal murder that to this day remains one of our nation's pivotal moments. The memory is etched forever in the minds of those old enough to remember where they were when they heard President Kennedy had been shot.

I was in my music class at my school, Stone Ridge, Convent of the Sacred Heart, when Mother Mahaney came to tell me the news. I immediately went home, where already many friends of my parents had gathered. I was too young to understand it fully, but I did realize that we had been struck by enormous loss. My normally loud and laughing home was now hushed.

I went upstairs to my parents' room and discussed what had happened with a great friend of my father, Dave Hackett. How could this have happened? Wasn't my uncle fighting the good fights—against communism and for civil rights, against poverty and for a more peaceful world? He'd inspired millions of young people across the globe with his call to service. How could his own public service not have been protected? Where was the God we prayed to every day to guide and protect Uncle Jack in his leadership? Did He know this had happened? Did He care?

On the day President Kennedy was buried, my father, Robert Kennedy, gave me a note he had handwritten that day. He was devastated. He had spent most of the time trying to comfort Aunt Jackie, and working out the vast logistics, protocol, and transition in the wake of his brother's death. But what he wrote to me did not convey fear, anger, or bitterness. He focused on the future and my duty to family and to our country. "Dear Kathleen, You seemed to understand that Jack died and was buried today. As the oldest of the Kennedy grandchildren—you have a particular responsibility now—a special responsibility to John [my cousin] and Joe [my brother]. Be kind to others and work for your country. Love, Daddy."

Can you imagine, in your own moment of unimaginable loss, reminding your child—and reminding yourself, really—to turn outward, not inward, to perform works of kindness and not of anger or revenge? It still stops my breath to think of him stealing away on that chaotic, dreadful day, for a quiet half-minute at his desk to make sure I would have this message with me always.

My father's message was very clear as he entrusted me with his sense of duty to family and to country. This duty was built on a foundation of Christian teachings about service to others and social justice. The promoters of that tradition, our priests and nuns, taught us weekly of the need to do good works in the world. And supporting them there was the entire Christian iconography, as interpreted by the Catholic Church, teaching us that the good life did not come just from following the rules and resisting temptations—after all, Jesus did not follow the rules—but from taking our faith out of our houses of worship and putting it into practice. And the more resources God had granted us, the more we were responsible to help those to whom less had been given. As Christians, we hold the suffering and agony of the Passion, death, and Resurrection of the Son of God at the very center of our faith. We reenact them every time we participate in the sacrifice of the Mass. These were miracles, but they are also guides for our own lives. The spirit in which we live will endure in the work we have done, and in the friends and foes we have made.

Even when I was twelve, the iconography and transcendent power of faith was as much a part of me as my lungs or my heart, and it provided me with a story to help me make sense of my uncle's death. In those immediate days and weeks after the assassination, I could not look at the image of Jesus without thinking of my uncle. No, he wasn't a saint, or the Son of God. But I could remember him sitting on the presidential yacht, named for his grandfather Honey Fitz, who had been a member of Congress and Boston's mayor, surrounded by family and friends, as he discussed the latest challenges in Washington—what to do about the segregationist Southern senators, or how to handle Soviet aggression in Berlin. My uncle's death had made me wonder why we should work for justice if justice was not to be given in return. But in thinking of the model of Jesus' life, I also was forced to embrace the model of Jesus' death. And in that, the tragedy of my uncle's death became bearable.

During the five years following Uncle John's assassination I watched my father carefully. In his immense sadness, he, too, wondered how and why this loss could have happened. How did God allow this? He wondered what he should do, what his public role should be. Could one's sense of duty be present if the universe made no sense? Through his years of searching for answers, my father resisted the temptation to despair, to be vengeful, to give in to bitterness. This was difficult for him. He was home much more than before, much more quiet and less energetic. He spent many hours in his room alone. But he prayed, read Greek poets and Shakespeare, looking first to understand fate, and only later to accept faith. He reminded himself that the ways of God are inscrutable, and that our mission from Him is earthbound, and focused on helping one another.

My uncle and my father had always been a team. Over time I witnessed my father emerging from his shattering loss to reengage in public life, this time alone. As he found his way through his grief, he grew in sympathy and sensitivity to the loss and pain he found in the lives of others. He became more tender in his actions and feelings for Americans who were caught up in the throes of the wrenching reckoning of the civil rights movement. Filled with a new awareness of emotional pain, he reached out to those who suffered—to the hungry and the exploited, to the neglected and the

ill, and to the weakest and most vulnerable among us—
the elderly and the children. Often he would quote the
French philosopher Albert Camus, "Perhaps we cannot
prevent this world from being a world in which children are tortured. But we can reduce the number of tortured children. And if you don't help us, who else in the
world can help us do this."

My father emerged from his private turmoil with a
public purpose, which as he said was "to seek a newer
world." He had taken to heart the notion that we are
here to help others, and he challenged his children to
take this to heart as well. Each of us, he believed, has
a moral obligation to pursue justice—not just putting
the bad guys in jail, but also making sure that the least
among us are treated with fairness.

My father became a voice for America's outrage at
the injustice of millions of citizens of the wealthiest
country on earth going hungry. He experienced his
anger when he saw migrant families who pick our
crops living in intolerably squalid conditions, working
incessantly and still unable to earn even a living wage.
He greeted the rage of African-Americans with empathy and understanding. He saw lives wasted in idleness
and isolation and was determined to rouse the fortunate and self-satisfied to moral action. He expressed
frustration that Americans lacked decent housing, effective public schools, and accessible health care and
in doing so awakened many Americans to the poverty

and hopelessness that had been invisible for so long. Finally, he was unable to bear that a good and decent country persisted in the killing of hundreds of thousands of innocent civilians, women, and children in a war that was being waged without wisdom in Southeast Asia. Americans needed leadership to lift them out of the despair and helplessness into which they'd sunk after the death of President Kennedy. In 1968, he ran for president.

In the midst of that campaign, when I was still in high school, my father was brutally murdered. Again, but this time even more personally and painfully, I grieved a death that instantly became part of the fabric of America's life and lore. I could not have imagined that the lessons in faith, hope, and love I'd so painfully absorbed after my uncle's death five years earlier would now be put to a harsher and even more agonizing test. And this time I'd bear this burden without my father at my side. Thankfully the power of my faith—and the central Christian experience of the death of innocence in the Passion and death of Jesus—came to me in a new and deeper way, emblazoned in my heart and soul. As a nation struggled with the loss, and in time sang songs portraying visions of my father walking the hills with "Abraham, Martin, and John," I prayed that I could find strength and hope in my faith, and love for myself and my country. "You have a particular responsibility now," my father had written to me on my uncle's death. "Be kind to others and work for your country." I needed to do that now, more than ever. But how?

Three weeks after my father died, I went to work on a Navajo Indian reservation in Rough Rock, Arizona. I had planned to go there in response to the challenge that my father had laid down in a speech at my high school earlier that year. He had pointed out that the unemployment rate was horrific on the reservation, that the teen suicide rate was the highest in the country, and that we in that high school were the lucky ones and had a responsibility to contribute.

My mother was wary of my leaving. She wanted me to stay at home in the comfort of my family. That might have been easier. I cried a lot that summer. But I wanted to be connected to my father's work, to his mission, and to his understanding that here on earth God's work must truly be our own. That meant caring for others, especially those whose lives offered them less opportunity than mine. It also meant bearing in mind constantly what was fair and just in society, and finding ways to speak out against apathy and indifference. It meant knowing not only that conditions in which some people live and work are unacceptable, but that I had a duty to get involved in making those conditions better. By his example, my father's life made clear that for any life to have meaning, it must include trying to improve the lot of our fellow human beings.

Sometimes I am nearly knocked over by the magnitude of my losses and the weight of the responsibility that was left to the next generation—to me. My uncle and my father were not saints, and neither am I. But their lives demonstrated the truths of Christian teachings— that in the paths we walk we should try to reduce the suffering and sadness of those whom we meet and, wherever we are given the opportunity, work for justice.

Churches could be the place to encourage, nurture, and promote this moral action. Except for sporting events, more people attend church than any other communal event in this country. About nine out of ten American adults claim that they believe in God. That's good news.

What's more, this passion has reached a remarkable height in our country today. Throughout history, faith has gone underground, only to emerge again in Great Awakenings, readying people for spiritual exploration. There are moments in history where people are ready and able to see the connection between the rituals of prayer and worship and the larger effort of improving God's world—and I believe we are now approaching just such a time. As a result, our churches and other centers of faith stand poised to provide a setting for genuine discussion of what a just society could look like, what we want our communities to be about, and what would make us worthy in our commitments to one another.

Yet there are also forces working against achieving our full potential. Are religious leaders sufficiently emphasizing the obligation engendered in faith to work for justice? Are they insisting that our nation could do a better job caring for the hungry and homeless—and showing the way to do so? Of course there are traditions that claim we are saved through faith alone; but even in those traditions, faith has translated into good works here on earth that, in the doing, help us understand why we are on earth, how we can live a good life, how we can make something meaningful of our days, and what is the best way to find happiness. In so doing, faith offers us the ability to resist temptation, to go beyond selfishness and empty materialism, and to find something that grips our souls. As in the Prophet Micah's words, our belief helps us "To do justice, and to love kindness, and to walk humbly with your God."

But these are fearful times. Few church leaders today connect religious teachings with a critique of the moral consequences of corporate greed, environmental degradation, failing schools, or lack of health care. Instead they preach—and Americans accept—a different and more privatized religion.

The term "privatized" might seem odd in this context, but it is a term for our times. I mean this in several ways. I mean that faith has become something you do personally, with eyes not toward earth but toward heaven, seeking a one-on-one experience with the divine. How many times have we talked about our "personal relationship with God"? Yes, everyone of faith strives for a connection to the divine. But too often we forget that this personal relationship can occur only through our connection to each person we meet. For it is they who carry the divinity within them.

Two interviews show just how far down this path the country has gone. In 1968, the British journalist David Frost interviewed my father and asked him, "What do you think we are on earth for?" My father answered,

> I think you have to break it down to people who have some advantages, and those who are just trying to survive and have their family survive. If you have enough to eat, for instance, I think basically it's to make a contribution to those who are less well off. "I complained because I had no shoes until I met a man who had no feet." You can always find someone that has a more difficult time than you do, has suffered more, and has faced some more difficult time one way or the other. If you've made some contribution to someone else, to improve their life, and make their life a bit more livable, a little bit more happy, I think that's what you should be doing.

My father was speaking from his perspective—a Catholic one to be sure, but one that would be easily understandable to those who practiced the Social Gospel.

That same year, when Frost asked then California governor Ronald Reagan the very same question, he answered,

> Well, of course, the biologist I suppose would say that like all breeds of animals, the basic instinct is to reproduce our kind, but I believe it's inherent in the concept that created our country—and in the Judeo-Christian religion—that man is for individual fulfillment; for our religion is based on the idea not of any mass movement but of individual salvation. Each man must find his own salvation; I would think that our national purpose in this country— and we have lost sight of it too much in the last three decades—is to be free—to the limit possible with law and order, every man to be what God intended him to be.

Ronald Reagan's words speak to many of us who understand the great value of a personal relationship with God. Feeling deeply that God loves you can help give you a sense that your life has purpose. That feeling can also give meaning to the toughest, darkest moments as God, all powerful and caring, holds you in His hands. It can give you a sense of inner peace, steadfastness, and confidence. But there are darker repercussions to Reagan's emphasis on the idea—central to conservative thought—that individual freedom is the root purpose of man (and, as it happens, of the American experiment as well). Out of this notion has grown an entire multimillion-dollar industry that treats God as little more than a self-help guru who helps you be all you can be. It smacks of Jesus' condemnation of the Pharisees, "For you are like whitewashed tombs, which outwardly appear beautiful, but within they are full of dead men's bones and all uncleanliness."

This instantly gratifying salvation can be mighty convenient. You can use your personal relation to give up drink, lose weight, and make money. It is a stunning and depressing reversal of the lesson I learned about our duty to God and country: As Charlie Peters, editor emeritus of *The Washington Monthly*, quipped, "Ask not what you can do for God, but what can God do for you?"

A darker side of this focus on private godliness is the right's total neglect of communal responsibility. Time after time, conservative policies, promoted in Washington with the language of "opportunity" and individual freedoms, have translated into disaster for the poor, the immigrant, and other disempowered groups, abandoned by the very government that should be protecting them. "Compassionate conservatism," it turned out, was just another way to put the wolf in sheep's clothing. Thirty-six million people are living in households where they do not know where their next meals are coming from. Poverty is on the rise.

But to blame politicians is too easy. Where have the churches been? What have they been teaching? If 81 percent of Americans call themselves Christian, what kind of Christianity blinds us to the needs of the homeless, the hungry, the stranger—the least among us?

Religion has also become privatized in its message: Today the moral lessons we hear—and the moral values we pursue in our politics—have everything to do with personal behavior. Living the moral life has come to mean something like: Don't have too much sex, gay sex, extramarital sex, premarital sex; don't have abortions; don't look at porn; don't demean marriage. (Not that many of us follow *all* these rules; there are more than a million abortions in this country each year, the highest divorce rates are in the most conservative parts of the country, and plenty of people of faith, including clergy, use pornography.)

Privatizing is a central theme of our times. Every day we hear public policy proposals for privatizing education through school vouchers and initiatives for privatizing Social Security, health care, and public lands and forests. Even "public" utilities such as water are being widely privatized. And our religious institutions have jumped on board, promoting a kind of privatized ambition and morality that works against the sense of communal good. The message seems to be, If it's good enough for me—or my family, or my tax bracket—then it's good enough.

My own Catholic Church has allowed its social agenda to be trumped by an all-consuming focus on contraception, abortion, same-sex marriage, and embryonic stem cell research—none of which are mentioned in the Gospels. Mainline Protestant churches have been losing members and power, and no longer serve as the voice for radical change—fighting for civil rights and against the Vietnam War—that they did only a generation ago. And evangelical Protestants—who have been fabulously successful in recruiting members—have focused their attention primarily on private matters: who has sex with whom, where, and how.

The Catholic Church of my youth dealt with issues at the core of the Gospel—suffering, injustice, sickness, and poverty. It provided me with a loving welcome when my father was killed. Its rituals, songs, stories of saints, and the Rosary led me out of my despair—just as they have helped countless others for two thousand years. My Church created a sense of community for family and friends that stretched back in time. The nuns who taught me had also taught my mother and the mothers of my friends and shared with us stories from times when they were as young as we. In many churches parishioners met regularly over bingo games, Sons of Italy dinners, and Christmas collections for the needy of the parish. The Church gave shape to our lives. It taught us how we should act at home, school, and work. And it taught us that how we acted locally was all part of God's larger plan for alleviating the suffering of humanity globally.

The very fact that the Church has endured for millennia across continents and cultures, under a variety of political systems, indicates that it has touched on something profound in the human spirit. This strength endures. Yet today, sadly, my Church seems focused primarily on protecting itself from the fallout of the pederasty scandal and publicizing its involvement in abortion politics. The first is a shame from which the Church will take a long time recovering. The second is an indication of its narrowing concerns. Here you have a group of men making decisions to ban contraception, and then turning around to demand that women must not have an abortion. These decisions do not affect them directly—they simply do not suffer the personal consequences. At least not yet. But this male hierarchy will eventually suffer from a female following that resents its decisions. Similarly it will suffer from its decision to keep women out of the hierarchy, to reject gays and lesbians, and to abandon its historic mission to the greater good of humanity.

My Church is building walls to keep the evil world out. This is not how it should be. I want my Church to be the embracing place that healed our souls while insisting that we live courageously and meaningfully in a world in which people near and far need our help. I want to return to the loving, caring Church that focused on helping people make sense of their lives by making a contribution to their larger community. If it is going to serve as Christ's voice in the twenty-first century, its theology must be able to handle the issues of today, including contraception, family planning, and the role of laity and of women both in the Church and society. People in the United States and throughout the world are looking for spiritual renewal. I want the Catholic Church to play its part.

Similarly I want the mainline Protestant churches to be able to speak to their congregations out of their proud history of personal and social engagement. The First Great Awakening, in the eighteenth century, led to the American Revolution, and the Second Great Awakening to the abolition of slavery and the granting of women's suffrage. Throughout our history determined Protestant congregations have made their mark by outlawing dueling, by supporting the temperance movement, the nineteenth-century women's movement, and the civil rights movement, by working to end child labor and to create the forty-hour workweek, by recognizing labor unions, and by speaking out against the war in Vietnam.

The leaders of these churches suffered the consequences of their bravery. For their actions on behalf of civil rights for blacks, and against the Vietnam War, they began to lose members and money, and they became afraid and cautious. But caution has not helped them either. Today, mainline churches are still losing members and money, and their political voice at the national level is weak. Worse yet, they simply are not speaking to the spiritual hunger in the country today. These churches must be able to reach into their rich history, back to a time when they were able to connect a personal relation to God with their congregants' efforts to improve the communities and nation in which they live. The strong communities of belief that once existed need to be revived.

The evangelical churches in some ways have the opposite problem: They touch people personally so they are growing by leaps and bounds; they have helped many people turn their lives around; they have created communities where members feel a great sense of connectedness and spirituality, and where they are given help with real-life issues—child care, schooling, marital counseling, aid for addictive behavior, and a safe place to meet a mate. And yet they, too, are building up walls of fear, protecting these "sacred" communities from the more profane influences of modern-day America. The debate over the teaching of evolution in schools, for instance, reflects the understandable fear of some religious people that morality cannot survive without a belief in God. I suspect, however, that it is yet another example of the right's determination to change the subject away from a discussion of our religious obligation to correct the inequities of our society.

Evangelical leaders have embraced a set of political priorities that is depressingly familiar and private: making abortion illegal, promoting anti-gay discrimination, fighting comprehensive sex education in favor of abstinence-only information—which has not proven to be an effective prevention against pregnancy—eliminating the teaching of evolution in schools, and reducing taxes. A slew of evangelical organizations promote themselves as "pro-family," which essentially begins and ends with trying to legislate in the arenas of personal and private morality. This is particularly ironic since evangelicals tend to also have a strong libertarian streak as well.

Among the most prominent evangelical leaders, personal morality is basically the alpha and omega of their concerns. Are they also concerned for social justice? Overseas, American evangelicals are a key force against human trafficking, slavery, and other human rights abuses. But here at home engagement in public issues like poverty, racism, and other forms of discrimination—issues that the Gospels clearly tell us Jesus cared about—are a low priority. Evangelical leaders would rather tick off a list of "thou shall nots" than work for progressive policies. Why are they fighting so hard against abortion instead of fighting to protect teenagers from the conditions that lead to unwanted pregnancy? Why are they promoting a message of hate and fear, rather than one of love and help? My faith teaches "Judge not, lest you be judged." And yet these churches seem satisfied to condemn others without offering help to solve the problem.

As a backdrop to all these sorry turns in our churches, political conservatives and liberals are engaged in an unholy—if inadvertent—alliance that has had the effect of further privatizing religion. For their own reasons, neither the left nor the right want churches to deal with public issues that revolve around economic unfairness and are reluctant to ask people of faith to call upon government to help shape a more just society. The right pretends that virtuous activity occurs only in the sphere of private behavior, not through governmental intervention. In fact they seem to think governmental intervention is appropriate only for overturning previous government decisions that they disagree with—e.g., the ban on school prayer—or in virtually anything having to do with what they consider improper sexual conduct, including homosexuality and abortion. The well-organized and politically attuned Religious Right pointedly ignores Christ's admonition that we should care for the "least among us" when it withdraws from those arenas where government has had a traditional role, such as enforcing civil rights, adjusting tax policy, and supporting social programs that can improve the daily lives of the poor.

Among leaders of the left, we find a different malady. They are obsessed with keeping religion out of the public sphere, demanding a perfect purging of faith from public life far beyond what our Founding Fathers meant by "separation of church and state." This obsession with secularism weakens their moral authority in mobilizing the national will to take on ingrained problems that stem from poverty and deprivation of civil rights. It makes the leaders of the left sound intellectual but without passion. The danger of not engaging religious teachings in the drive for social reform might be worse than condemning them. Reason and rationality alone will not usher in a new era of honesty, social justice, protection of the earth, and respect for women. It just won't happen. Like addiction to drugs or alcohol, one cannot eliminate a behavior simply by arguing that it is destructive. The successful fight against addiction requires a deep hope and faith in something greater than oneself.

For the left, making judgments about personal behavior may be uncomfortable. But it is necessary if we are to have a moral leg to stand on. It means acknowledging that conservatives are correct on some issues: that welfare reform was not the disaster that was predicted and in fact had some good results, that pornography in the age of an Internet so easily accessed by our children is more than a personal option, that promiscuity on today's college campuses is a problem for the young people who are engaging in it. And it means pushing further than the right on some issues: for instance, insisting that no one of any political or religious stripe has given sufficient attention and voice to the problems of drug abuse and underage drinking. Would it be so wrong to draw some moral lines in the liberal sand?

Neither the left nor the right seems willing to acknowledge that there is an appropriate role for religious teachings in illuminating what would be required, as expressed in the Preamble to the Constitution, to "provide for the common defense, promote the general welfare, and secure the blessings of liberty to ourselves and our posterity." On the complicated questions of how best to care for the least among us—the poor, the immigrant, the disabled veteran—religious teachings appear to be about the last place we look for wisdom. Yet these are questions on which we desperately need such guidance.

Finding the proper relationship between religion and politics has always been among the most divisive of debates in America. And for good reason. At times, religion and politics have been mixed in a way that debases both. When explicit or implicit religious tests are used to determine whether someone is fit to hold office; when theological differences are cast into public policy; or when voters are told that one party is godly while another is not, we are belittling both faith and public life.

But on a broader scale, we must not miss the essential connection between religion and politics. Both religion and politics aspire to create a better world, and both emphasize the importance of realizing our connection to one another. In faith, we are bound to one another through our Creator, whose image we reflect. In politics, we are bound to one another through our shared faith that all "are created equal." There can be no doubt that our greatest moments have come when we were able to overcome division and work together to build a more just society.

Faith's essential contribution to our political life must be to offer an enduring vision of connection to one another. Jesus asked us to love our neighbor as ourselves and to see His face in the face of strangers. By working to improve the lives of others, we not only move closer to God, but we move our country closer toward the vision of our Founding Fathers.

I believe many Americans yearn for a public ethic, one that reconciles the wisdom contained in the First Amendment of the Constitution with the values of religious faith. The First Amendment prohibits the state establishment of religion and protects one's ability to practice one's religion, and both these rights must be respected and preserved. Whereas we often talk about the wall separating religion and government, my sense is that a wall is the wrong metaphor; a window would be more appropriate. Religion stands on one side of the window, but it can provide the understanding and motivation to act on the other side. The question is how to achieve this. To find the answer, we must examine what we have lost and try to recover the community spirit that has been at the heart of religious observance in this country.

We must learn to treat all people as our neighbors, and love them as ourselves. We share so much. We share in God's creation and in His blessings. We all have hopes and dreams. All yearn for a life of purpose. And each of us at different times is confronted with the death of loved ones, with disappointment, with sadness. Still, we can each know the courage of our fellow human beings who deal bravely with sickness, find satisfaction in some success, in finding love, in serving others, in leaving the world better.

It is up to us to be a good neighbor in the literal and biblical sense, in acts of compassion both large and small, and to try to improve those public places and services so that the public welfare can be served and neighbors we don't see can enjoy the liberty that comes from knowing that the schools are good, health care is available, the environment safe and healthy.

We can certainly all agree that we are called to protect the earth for future generations; that we should not elect a government that favors the rich over the poor with tax breaks and other benefits; that we cannot allow ourselves to fear our neighbor and therefore that we must fight violence, gangs, and drug use; that discrimination against and oppression of any group—be they minorities, gays, women, or anyone else—is an un-American conduct we cannot abide. There are so many routes in the pursuit to justice, and my hope is that you will choose one of them. I promise that if you do, you will begin to transform the world. I found that to be true for my father, for Martin Luther King Jr., Dorothy Day, César Chávez, Philip and Daniel Berrigan. And I've seen its transformative power with so many around the world—Archbishop Desmond Tutu, Lech Walesa, Andrei Sakharov, and the *comadres* in El Salvador. These are heroes on a superhuman scale. We may not match their efforts, and we may become discouraged along the way, just as they did, but these are not reasons for us not to try.

I write this book as a way of sharing what my faith has meant to me, but more important, as a way of reminding us how the United States has been shaped by progressive religious traditions. At its best, this tradition has made America a more inclusive, just, and fair nation. Christians and non-Christians alike can learn from this tradition to understand how faith can serve to unify our country, rather than divide it. Our history is rich with inspiring stories. In thinking about the barriers to living out those traditions today, I offer suggestions on how the churches in this era can link the most profound of their teachings to the unsolved problems of our time. I write about how women's lives intersect with the church and with its teachings, and I focus on individuals—many of whom are personal heroes of mine due to the extraordinary moral example of their lives—who can also help point the way. My hope is that each of us is able to see our best selves reflected in those who have gone before us and will decide to take action in ways that are most needed, whether in our families, churches, communities, or in politics.

When I was young I thought of becoming a nun, but by the time I was twelve years old, I knew that wasn't going to be my path. Yet I also was sure that I would always ask myself if I was doing God's work here on earth. This is the message the Bible offers us. The Scriptures remind us not only that we must love God and that God loves us, but that we must love our neighbor. The Scriptures insist not only that we have a responsibility to create a better spiritual *self*, but that the spiritual self is inextricably combined with the mission of creating a more just community, society, and world.

The teachings of all religious traditions have always emphasized sacrifice, duty, caring for the least among us, and loving our neighbor. Once we feel connected to those who share our world, we cannot be truly free so long as there are those who are hungry, sick, and living under oppression. Improving our own lives with goods, power, publicity—even with a spiritual connection to God—is not enough. Each of us wants to know whether what we've done has made life better for others. This aspiration is part of the human condition, as is underscored in my Catholic tradition. We all suffer, and our suffering can take us into ourselves, our family, our group, or our suffering can open us to the suffering of others outside our immediate circle. Greater love hath no man than he who gives up his life for his friends, but the fact is that Jesus gave up His life for generations unknown to Him. If we aspire to give as Jesus did, we will find that our hearts are opened to others, so that we are moved to render goodness unto our fellow human beings.

This is hard work, but it is also work that brings untold joy in the effort. I have often thought how fortunate I am to be in a position to make a difference, to feel part of a cause greater than myself, and to be doing worthy work. There may be a sportslike competitive aspect to all of this. Certainly in the heat of the fight, I feel my own blood rising in the effort to win. But if part of human nature is to improve, better ourselves, and develop our skills—so much the better. Battling the forces of evil and working for social justice can be the ultimate self-help. Action in service to others can be the path to satisfaction and salvation. Let us begin the journey.

CHAPTER TWO

Much Is Expected

During the course of writing this book, one week stands out. Twice that week I was asked if I was a nun. The first time was at a funeral, and the nun who asked thought she remembered me from a convent experience years before. In fact she had simply seen me over and over on television while I was running for governor of Maryland. The second time was on a plane. My seatmate noticed that I was reading a book about Catholicism. She was a farmer from Texas, wearing bathroom slippers, about sixty years old. She grew up Roman Catholic, she told me. The Church had "helped me be good," she said, but explained that she was "not the confessing type" and had left the Church because it had not been good to her. It had made her feel guilty, like God was always looking down on her from His perch in heaven, judging her, making her feel inadequate. "Who needs that?" she said.

I told her that no, I was not a nun, but I was a Catholic because the Church had been good to me. In recalling our exchange a few days later, I thought my answer had been too reflexive. Why am I a Catholic? Why had I said the Church had been good to me? I could just as easily make the opposite case. Certainly the Church had attacked me, tried to isolate me, and generally tried to make me feel unwelcome. This could be said of many otherwise loyal Catholics who have been angered and alienated by the Church's aggressive stance on birth control, divorce, abortion, but my complaint was more specific: The Church's attacks had been personal. I had been criticized because I am from a prominent Catholic family and took a pro-choice stance on abortion when I ran for political office. Priests preached against me from the pulpit. My own archdiocese blacklisted me from speaking. And when I did speak at Catholic events, I was picketed—called "baby killer" and greeted by signs asking, "How can you call yourself a Catholic?"

The first time this happened, I felt as if members of my own family were attacking me, trying to deny my kinship and my faith. But over the years, my perspective has changed. I no longer focus on individual opponents, and as a result I no longer take the Church's attacks personally. Instead, I see the problem lies with a Church intent on protecting its own powers and privileges from the outside world rather than living out Christ's message of truth, forgiveness, and love. And if those "outside" elements include Catholics who desire change—Catholics like me—then the Church is determined to keep us out as well.

I believe this cannot be God's will. God's Church should be a welcoming Church, not a rejecting one. Even if we people of faith disagree on some political and scientific questions, are we not supposed to hunger and thirst for justice? My Church is in need of reform and I pray that it comes.

So why did I answer that the Church has been good to me? Because it has been my spiritual home. It has nurtured my faith in God and shaped my understanding of why we are on earth. And it has transmitted to me four valuable, intertwined messages: that we are loved by God; that we must fight evil both in ourselves and in the world; that we are connected in a mystical way to all humanity and are therefore obligated to seek out and repair the suffering of our fellow human beings; and that we must pursue justice, especially for the poor. By teaching that we are all children of God, that I am my neighbor's keeper, the Church taught me that I must make an effort to know my neighbors and to be open to their struggles, their sufferings, their hopes and dreams. I am called to seek justice and in that cause to be prepared to sacrifice myself for others. My faith gives me the determination to act with integrity, and the humility to know that there is always more to learn and to do.

It is the intertwining of those messages that I most love about the Church: its pursuit of personal salvation and its recognition that we neither suffer nor are saved alone. This has made many Catholics into good citizens, and it has made the Church itself into a good global citizen, pursuing social justice, human rights, and peace. The fact that today it has strayed from those roots does not change the moral strength it has given to me and to the world.

I grew up the oldest of eleven children at the most marvelous moment in our country's history for Catholics. The old stereotype of Catholics as ignorant and superstitious was being put to rest. My uncle John F. Kennedy had become the first Catholic president, thus overcoming the prejudice that many Protestants harbored against Catholics—that we could not think on our own, that we were subservient to the Pope, and that we were not real Americans. At the same time, Pope John XXIII was reaching out to a welcoming world with the launching of Vatican II. He would show that Catholics endorsed freedom of religion, democracy, and political freedom.

Perhaps because I grew up at a time when being Catholic was something to be proud of, I have always accepted Catholicism as part of who I am. I am a Catholic in the way that I am a member of my family or an American. Just as my family raised me, shaped me, taught me, provided me with a sense of rootedness, so has Catholicism. And just as being an American means being part of a nation born of great hopes and often devastating mistakes, so, too, Catholicism has a muddled history that evokes both pride and a determination to reform.

Religion was very alive to us. This faith grew from the experiences of my grandmothers. My mother's mother, Ann Brannack Skakel, was a devout Catholic, fascinated by the saints and the cloistered monks at Gethsemani. She passed her strong faith on to her children, whose homes were filled with images of Our Lady, statues of the suffering Christ, and an abiding commitment to the Church. My father's mother, Rose, went to Mass daily during the week and twice on Sundays. She described how her faith helped her get through the tough times in her life by saying she believed that God would never give you something that you could not handle. Her Catholicism also had a strong cultural component. She would describe how even when her father was mayor of Boston, the Protestant powers never respected Catholics—thought them boozing, womanizing roughnecks.

Like Grandmother Rose, my mother went to Mass every day. During the summer, when most children played ball or at least slept in, she took along the old-est five or six of us children to 8:00 Mass—every single morning. We went to St. Francis Xavier in Hyannis—about a five-minute drive from where we lived. It was packed on Sundays, but during the week there were usually fewer than twenty other worshippers. We were generally late. It wasn't easy to rouse us from bed morning after morning, get us all dressed in decent out-fits, and pile us into the convertible along with the dogs. But to make up for the time we missed my mother would stay to say more prayers after the Mass ended.

I liked going to Communion, and I liked the feeling that Jesus was with me and would protect me through-out the day. St. Francis was a lovely church, with its heavy oak pews, rough-hewn stone walls, soaring ceil-ings, and stained glass windows depicting stories from the Bible and the Stations of the Cross. The Mass in those days was still in Latin, the priest mostly had his back toward us, and the ritual was full of mystery. Even before I could read and follow the Mass, I would stare at the windows, feel the warmth of Our Lady looking down on me, wonder at how incredible it would be to walk on water, and shiver at the thought of Jesus en-during His suffering and torment.

As a Catholic girl in a family of eleven children the issues that would prove challenging in my adult years were far away. We were not conflicted in our faith. We carried it with us everywhere. My mother infused our home with Catholic spirit. Each bedroom had a special holder for holy water and a statue of Mary or a picture of the crucifix. The room that my brother Bobby (Robert Francis) shared with David and Michael had fifteen pictures depicting the life of St. Francis. It turned out that Francis was an appropriate middle name for Bobby. By the age of six he could name a hundred reptiles, and he would grow up to become a prominent environmentalist.

My parents insisted that we pray each morning, and before and after every meal. At night we gathered for evening prayers, either at my parents' bed or at the top of the stairs. We recited the traditional nighttime prayer, "Now I lay me down to sleep," then prayed for all the members of our family, said the Rosary, and asked that John Kennedy be the best president and Daddy the best attorney general ever.

Our imaginations were shaped by the images that pervaded our faith. There was God the Father, who was at times difficult to deal with because He was God, He was perfect, and He was judging us. It was always hard to understand how He could ask Abraham to sacrifice his son. This was not a story to imbue children with the love of God! Jesus was loving, but a little intimidating. By contrast, Mary, the mother of God, and the saints were our intimates, helping us daily in both mundane and holy ways. My mother had a particular devotion to St. Anthony, who was the patron saint of things lost and found. We were always praying to St. Anthony to find a parking space whenever we went to the movies, or shopping, or to visit my father at the Senate, or pick him up at the airport. And St. Anthony always came through. In fact he was so successful that my brother David was given the middle name Anthony in his honor.

On many evenings we listened as our mother read stories from *Sixty Saints for Girls* or *Sixty Saints for Boys*, or a chapter from the Bible (always the Old Testament). The saints always seemed to be getting tortured for their faith—thrown to the lions, drowned, hanged, executed with arrows, or burned at the stake like Joan of Arc. These stories underscored the message that you weren't always going to be popular if you tried to do the right thing. There were always people who would criticize you, and try to hurt you, if not kill you. I remember my father saying that one could be judged by the enemies that one made. The point was clear: A good life was not a popularity contest.

When it came time for the coming-of-age sacrament of confirmation, we were prepared for the moment when we would choose a saint to be our model. Joe, ever the contrarian, chose the patriarch Jacob rather than a saint. Joe was inspired by the story of Jacob wrestling with God. My parents were not happy with his choice. I suspect that they would have preferred something more traditional. But I thought then and still think now that Joe's choice was appropriate: Joe challenges authority and is great in the trenches. I chose St. Theresa the Little Flower. She was a nineteenth-century French nun who wrote about how we can do God's work by acts of kindness. She seemed like a good model for more modern times because her ministry was helping people rather than being a martyr. I did not plan to be burned or beheaded.

My mother made sure that my godfather was Dr. Danny Walsh, her theology professor at Manhattanville College of the Sacred Heart. She deeply respected Danny and wanted his holiness to bless her new family. (He is mostly known for his role in helping to convert Thomas Merton to Catholicism.) When I was growing up, I knew that Danny Walsh was thinking about me, and for every Christmas he sent a fruitcake made by the monks of the Abbey of Gethsemani, where he had chosen to teach after leaving Manhattanville. In class or in church, I often thought, "Dr. Danny is praying for me." He was telling me to find out what God wanted me to do, and to try to be a good person.

Sadly, we had many tragic reasons to rely on our faith as I was growing up. Death has always been near. I was named for my aunt Kathleen, who died in a plane crash before I was born, and my brother Joe was named for our uncle who was killed in World War II. At every Mass and every evening we would pray for them. My mother's parents were added to those prayers when I was four years old, after they, too, were killed in a plane crash. When I was fourteen, my mother's brother George Skakel was killed in another plane accident along with one of my father's best friends, Dean Markham. Nine months later my aunt Pat, George's wife, died choking on a chicken bone. In college, one of my best friends died from a gunshot wound.

I remember going to wakes, attending funerals, and comforting cousins and friends. Each time someone died, our faith gave us strength. We had a wake, prayed the Rosary, and went to Mass. The Church had shaped our habits of mourning and a belief that our uncle or aunt or friend was with God in heaven. To the uninitiated this may sound like gobbledygook or fairy tales. But to those like me who experienced the rituals time and time again, they gave shape to a very difficult and sad situation. And those habits—the belief in redemption, the hope that we could all be together in heaven—eased the terrible sense of loss. They also reminded us that we were supposed to live each day doing as much kindness and goodness as we could, since each day might be our last.

This message came through even in less tragic times. My parents often quoted St. Luke: "To whom much is given, much is expected." They also quoted parts of Matthew 25: "As you did it to one of the least of these my brethren, you did it to me." My father emphasized this for my brothers, sisters, and me in very personal ways. I remember one time when he had been away in Mississippi for a few days and returned home on a Saturday night. It was a beautiful spring evening. We had sat down to dinner in the dining room, with the crystal chandelier hanging from the ceiling, the table set with a linen tablecloth and china. He talked to us about the Delta. "Families there live in a shack the size of this dining room," he said. "The children have distended stomachs and sores all over them because they don't have enough food. Do you know how lucky you are, do you know how lucky you are? Do something for our country. Give something back."

I learned early on the lesson that faith is tough, that it is not meant to give comfort to the comfortable but to make us ask each day: Can I do more? Am I doing my best? Am I using the talents that God gave me? Am I making the world a better place?

And I learned at an early age that giving back isn't always easy. When I was twelve years old, a friend and I delivered a Christmas dinner to a family living in a tenement building in inner-city Washington. We walked up three flights of narrow, poorly lit stairs to deliver turkey, stuffing, vegetables, and a bag of toys. After a little boy greeted us at the door, his mother quickly came, thanked us, took the packages, and then we left. The entire exchange took less than five minutes. I still recall the vaguely embarrassed feeling I had as I walked down the stairs. Were they resentful of my good fortune? Had I made the mother feel inadequate because she had not provided for her children? And what about us? Were our motives for volunteering pure, or was I just trying to make myself feel better for having come from such a fortunate family?

These were provocative questions. But I wanted to make sure that questioning my motives would not serve as an excuse for inaction, for not trying to make things better. One of the most important things about Catholic life is that you're never supposed to be completely comfortable. We were always taught to serve, but also taught never to be fully satisfied. Regardless of our own feelings, we were obligated to make the effort. While it is easy to dismiss the visit as just another example of Lady Bountiful, the bottom line is that there was a fine result. The family had a real Christmas dinner. Whatever discomfort we may have felt delivering the meal was irrelevant compared to the good that was accomplished. I understood that while at school it might be interesting to discuss the "deserving" poor, the Christ of the New Testament told us to feed the least of our little ones.

I always wondered how even people like me could get to heaven if it was easier for a camel to get through the eye of a needle than for a wealthy person to be saved. Years later when I visited Israel, I was told that the "eye of the needle" was a gate in Jerusalem that was difficult for a camel to pass though but not impossible. When I told my mother, she said that she preferred the original interpretation. Even when given an out, she nonetheless chose the psychic space that was familiar—moral discomfort. I admired her for not trying to make the story easy on herself. As we've seen, from time to time strains of Christianity come into vogue that view wealth as a sign of God's approbation, that link success in this world with portents of heaven in the next. That was certainly not my mother's way.

The lessons that I learned about my obligations to others were reinforced in the Catholic schools I attended from kindergarten through tenth grade, from 1956 through 1967. From first through fourth grade, I went to parochial school at Our Lady of Victory in Washington, D.C., where we had forty-five kids in our class and played on the church parking lot for recess. Today parents and educational advocates insist that children should learn in small classes—of fewer than twenty-five students. I am sure they are right. I always thought that the nuns could handle this much larger number because they had the hope of heaven and the threat of hell to keep us in line. In fifth grade I changed schools to attend Stone Ridge, Convent of the Sacred Heart in Maryland, which had much smaller classes. It was there that I learned some of the most important lessons of my childhood.

The convent, an all-girls school, sat on a beautiful wooded hill on thirty-five acres of carefully mowed grass and was taught by the same order of nuns that had taught my mother and my aunts. Perhaps the most haunting image I came away with after my ten years of

Catholic education was St. Paul's notion that we are all part of the mystical body of Christ. I saw myself as one cell in a great body—connected to everyone else in a way known only to our Creator. I imagined myself sharing a common humanity, not only with kids like myself, living in lovely Northwest Washington and its suburbs, but with people living all over the world.

The nuns of Sacred Heart made sure that we grasped the notion of "baptism of desire," which taught that there was salvation outside the Church—those who use "natural reason" to seek God and reject evil can be in a state of grace. The Church in Her wisdom envisioned a God who wanted all to be saved, not just those lucky few who had grown up in a particular culture in a particular time in history. The practice of our faith was to be proletarian, populist, democratic.

Self-discipline was a critical part of becoming a strong muscle in the mystical body. For us children that meant obedience, and it infused our education. We made confession weekly. We were required to walk in silence to class, sit silently before class began, and silently stand in the lunch line. Our report cards, in addition to math, English, and geography, included grades for fortitude, respect, seriousness of purpose, and whether we helped build a strong community—a category then called "intercourse with companions." (I hear that particular wording is no longer included.)

I have heard from Catholic pals who have attended

other schools that the nuns they knew were often mean, intimidating, and scary. But that was not my experience. To me, Stone Ridge was a welcoming place—a kind of second home. The nuns were more mysterious than frightening. They lived in the "cloistered" part of the school, where no layperson was allowed to set foot. They wore long dark habits with big crosses. My mother had actually attended high school and college with some of the nuns. They had given up their comfortable lives of lovely homes, possibly handsome husbands, and beautiful clothes for God. They were admirable. They were doing what all of us could be doing but did not have the courage, or the dedication, or the commitment to do. I wanted their goodness, their purity of heart to rub off on me—without of course having to give up all that they were willing to sacrifice.

At Stone Ridge, we were often told the story of Mother Duchesne, who was renowned for her courageous decision to become a missionary to the Native Americans. She braved the terrors of frontier life, icy winters, bare quarters, loneliness, and hardship in territories near the Mississippi River. But what was always most impressive was how she would pray all night long with absolute concentration. Native American children would place leaves on her habit in early evening, go to bed, and rise early in the morning, and see that the leaves had not moved at all, so engrossed was she in her prayers. Let me tell you, if you are constantly reminded of the story of Mother Duchesne, it makes it much easier to stand quietly in line at school, or to go out into the world to do good works and fight evil.

Those evils we were to fight were not theoretical in any sense. They were real, and they were trying to do us wrong, like Jimmy Hoffa, whom my father had investigated as part of the Senate Rackets Committee. My father came home after battling corruption in the Teamsters union. He said, "Either they will own the country or we will." The stakes were made very clear to me. At one point during my father's investigation, Hoffa threatened to throw acid in my eyes. Every afternoon, I had to wait after school in the principal's office until my mother arrived to take me home. I waited on the second floor watching my classmates flood onto the pavement while I watched for my mother to arrive in the white convertible to pick me up. Before I went to school my mother used to bring my brother Joe and me to the Rackets Committee hearings, where we watched men take the Fifth and refuse to answer my father's questions. It was always clear to me from a very young age that there were people who disobey the law and do terrible things. The fact that we could not leave school with the other children simply affirmed my sense that life was a struggle.

I also learned that evil had been our enemy during World War II. Often Father Richard McSorley from

Georgetown University would come for dinner. After tutoring my brothers he would stay for dinner and recount his experiences in the Pacific Theater, the Bataan Death March, and the terrible tortures that our soldiers were subjected to. Godless communism was another enemy. My father described the terrible living conditions and lack of freedom that he had witnessed on his trip to the Soviet Union in 1955. Every Mass ended with a prayer for the conversion of those behind the Iron Curtain.

But we also learned that evil was not limited to corrupt union presidents, businesses, or governments. We were taught to take on the evils of poverty: hunger, homelessness, and illness. One of my friend's uncles was a missionary Maryknoll priest in Chol-Chol, Chile. Naturally enough our class "adopted" him, raised money for the village where he worked, sent clothes, and felt connected to his work. It was clear that we were to help regardless of whether people were baptized Catholic or not. And, to their credit, the nuns could also find the good in communistic ideals. In fact, the nuns even saw some wisdom in the communism our country hated.

Once, I asked a teacher why, if communism was so terrible, it was so widespread around the world. In direct contrast to the prevailing sentiments of the time, the teacher refused to demonize the idea of communism or the people living in communist countries. Even though communism was essentially atheistic, she explained, many of the values that we were taught to admire in our nuns and priests were the same as those of communism. No one owns property here, she told me. We share everything. She said that this was also how the early disciples lived. Considering the depth of the animosity to communism in the country then, in the late 1950s, her answer was courageous. (In retrospect, it's possible to see why there was such hostility to Catholicism. Not many Catholics were pro-communist, but Catholicism did not celebrate individualism as strongly as others might have wished.)

My father liked to say that priests were Republicans and nuns Democrats, and so he felt a special affection for these women of God. What my peers and I learned from the nuns was the importance of living for something greater than yourself. When the mother superior of my grammar school, Mother Mouton, asserted that each of us had to develop our talents for the greater glory of God, we believed her. Obedience, even in a convent, was not the only virtue. She told us, "Silence is golden. But sometimes it's just plain yellow." Whispered rumors that Mother Mouton had once been a Mardi Gras queen and an attorney—and gave it up to join the convent—gave credence to her sermon that whatever our vocation would be, we had a responsibility to work hard for the well-being of the community. She had given up a successful life in the world in order to devote herself to God and to education. She inspired us. Even if we could not match her sacrifices, we should always ask ourselves what we could be doing better. Her life, like the stories of the saints, was not simply an amusing tale: It was a standard to which all of us needed to aspire.

My father walked his days with the suffering of the less fortunate on one shoulder and the Catholic teachings of social justice on the other, a friend once told me. Alice Roosevelt Longworth said, "Bobby Kennedy could have been a revolutionary priest." My grandmother Rose believed that my father was the most religious boy in the family of nine—five girls and four boys. Dick Goodwin, an aide to John Kennedy, said my father was "the Christian among the brothers, the one who is the believer."

It was Catholic tradition in particular that helped my father dramatically sharpen his sense of justice, which is why it so outraged him when he saw powerful forces acting in ways that were neither fair nor just. It didn't matter whether it was Dave Beck and Jimmy Hoffa ripping off the Teamsters, the police who arrested Martin Luther King Jr. for a traffic violation, the sheriff who jailed César Chávez's compatriots to "prevent them from doing anything wrong," or the oil companies in South America who underpaid the local workers and wrecked the environment. To him, each injustice represented a clear threat to people's ability to fulfill our God-given gifts.

The obligation my father felt was not merely abstract—you could see the passion in all his interactions. He had a great sense of justice. He knew that we were to live lives of purpose and meaning, and that we, the more fortunate, had a greater burden. So he could come home from work angry at the recalcitrance of the Southern power structure and unhappy if he suspected that his children had not tried their best. He liked to tell us that on the walls of the pyramids there was a scribbled note, "and no one was angry enough to speak out." He had an amazing gift for empathy. He listened to leaders in the African-American community who had been discriminated against and humiliated by an unjust legal and economic system. Hardly a week goes by without someone telling me a personal story of how he was able to understand their troubles and their dreams, comfort them, and inspire them to serve their community and their country.

The day that Martin Luther King Jr. was killed, my father was on his way to deliver a speech in Indianapolis during his campaign for president. He received word of Dr. King's death, and then a message from Mayor Richard Lugar that he should not come to give the speech, as the city could not guarantee his safety. The mayor was not being unreasonable. Across the country, cities had broken out in rioting after hearing the news. But my father believed that he had to go. His campaign was about reconciliation. On his way he scribbled a few notes.

He stood on the back of a flatbed truck and told the crowd of Dr. King's death. They had not heard the news. After the gasps of grief and lost hope, he delivered a speech that, sadly, still resonates today:

> My favorite poet was Aeschylus. And he once wrote, "Even in our sleep, pain which cannot forget falls drop by drop upon the heart until, in our own despair, against our will, comes wisdom through the awful grace of God."
>
> What we need in the United States is not division, what we need in the United States is not hatred; what we need in the United States is not violence and lawlessness; but is love, and wisdom, and compassion toward one another, and a feeling of justice toward those who still suffer within our country, whether they be white or whether they be black.
>
> So I shall ask you tonight to return home, to say a prayer for the family of Martin Luther King, that's true, but more importantly to say a prayer for our own country, which all of us love—a prayer for understanding and that compassion of which I spoke.

While more than a hundred cities broke out in riots that night, there were none in Indianapolis. A black assistant chief of police said that the senator and his family could have slept outside all night, and remained unharmed. My father had reached people with his own understanding of suffering and pain and with what had been his clear determination to serve and to help. His actions gave his words credibility.

The oppression of African-Americans was not just unfortunate, or even a political problem to be solved. It was a moral question, and the search for solutions to it was imperative, not optional. In South Africa in 1966 he said, "It is not realistic or hardheaded to solve problems and take action unguided by ultimate moral aims and values . . . In my judgment, it is thoughtless folly. For it ignores the realities of human faith and of passion and belief—forces ultimately more powerful than all of the calculations of our economists and of our generals."

He grasped the critical insight that knowing what is right does not always lead to right action. To overcome fear, despair, apathy, and indifference—to screw up the courage needed to act out a life of moral courage—requires a heartfelt commitment. For many, faith in a loving and just God provides that impetus.

After he returned home from South Africa, my father wrote an article for *Look* magazine attacking the legal institutions of racism, both at home and abroad. He titled it "Suppose God Is Black?" He saw that one of the best ways to challenge moral complacency was to invoke God—and not the God that always approves of our actions. (How different would be the church's position regarding women if we took seriously that admonition that God is neither female nor *male*!)

My father was eager to ask how we solve the injustice of poverty. How do we make our country more just and more equitable for everyone? But his answer was more complex than "social justice." He believed strongly in personal responsibility. He understood that each of us yearns not just for economic well-being but also for a sense of pride in what we have accomplished. He criticized the welfare system for failing to provide a way for those who are given the handout to say to themselves and to their fellow citizens, "I have made a contribution, I am not invisible." He opposed the guaranteed annual income for the same reasons. In short, his was a Catholic sensibility.

Sadly, the path of the Catholic Church and its teachings has turned sharply in another direction since the 1960s. Today the church hierarchy does not provide the inspiration and moral strength that my father and so many others were able to draw on years ago.

The early 1960s had been a time of great pride in Catholicism and hope for the future. A Catholic had been elected president of the most powerful country in the world, and the Catholic Church itself seemed poised for progressive change. In 1962, Pope John XXIII launched Vatican II, only the second ecumenical council since the Council of Trent in the sixteenth century.

He hoped to bring the Church into the modern era "with Joy and Hope." While retaining its commitment to those elements of church doctrine that attracted so many throughout the centuries—the belief in the incarnation, the forgiveness of sins, the resurrection of the dead, and life in the world to come—the Vatican Council made clear that God works though history and that the Church must be able to adapt to the times.

The documents produced at Vatican II made explicit that Catholics are not to be separate from a fallen world, but to see the world as God's marvelous creation in which we are to do His work. We are not to be so fearful of temptation that we need to ward ourselves off from society or rely on the hierarchy to tell us, the laity, what to do. Just the opposite: the laity gained new recognition. Rules were changed so that it was easier for us to participate: We were not just to be lectured at by the all-knowing, all-holy priest. The altar was reversed so that the priest looked at the parishioners and we in turn could look right back. We lay Catholics would write new songs, redo the marriage ceremony, receive Communion from women, and watch girls serve at Mass. One document announced that the laity are "priest and prophet," a principle that even today empowers the laity in their arguments with the hierarchy.

Vatican II broke new ground for the Church. It encouraged dialogue with other religions. It promoted Communion by removing the three-hour fasting requirement and asserting that going to Mass on Saturday could meet one's Sunday obligation. And at Vatican II, two centuries late, the Vatican finally agreed that the idea of freedom of religion in the American meaning made sense. Finally all those Catholic politicians had the Pope's explicit blessing.

I don't know whether my father did this in response to Vatican II or whether he was simply feeling the spirit of the times, but in the early 1960s my father started to read the Bible to his children in conjunction with our evening prayers. When I reported this to my grandmother Rose, she was surprised. "Catholics don't read the Bible," she said. This was a gross generalization, of course. But it touched on a truth about Catholics. We relied on our priests and the Church hierarchy to read and interpret the Bible. But after Vatican II, that began to change. The Catholic laity was being acknowledged and recognized.

Still, for every step forward, there was another, more conservative element in the Church pulling it two steps back. And these elements found their opening to drag the Church back to its more moralistic ways in the sexual revolution.

It was just at this juncture that I, too, was coming of age. In 1968, my father was killed. I was in high school then, and during the next few years, in so many ways, I would have to grow up. Part of that growing meant dealing with the sexual questions in my own life, just as the country itself was challenging its historical sexual "innocence," and just as my Church was being pushed to respond.

The Church at that time proved of little help. Rather than develop a subtle and nuanced attitude about the use of contraceptives, it kept to its age-old teaching. No, no, no: not in use before marriage, not in marriage to prevent conception, not even if the wife's life could be put in danger with another pregnancy. During this period, many had hoped that the Church would change its position on birth control. Other Christian denominations that had previously condemned contraception now approved it. But in 1968 Pope Paul VI issued *Humanae Vitae*, condemning birth control. Men and women who had grown up in the Church and had once trusted their Church were confronted with the awful choice of no sex or more children—or of disobeying their Church. Forty years later, a friend still shakes and goes red in his face as he recounts going to the priest to explain that at the age of twenty-one he already had three children and simply could not afford to care for more. The priest was stern, stubborn, and unsympathetic: "Your parents could do it. So should you." The conclusion was obvious: The Church cared more about its tradition than its flock. That theme would be repeated over and over again in the coming years.

The massive disregard of *Humanae Vitae* among the clergy as well as the laity should have been fair warning to Rome that something was amiss. Within the decade, and after the 1973 *Roe v. Wade* Supreme Court decision, the issue of abortion had to be addressed in the Church. A number of Catholic leaders such as Father Robert Drinan suggested that the Church refrain from taking a political position on abortion on the grounds that all moral issues need not be legislative ones. But the hierarchy in Rome refused that stance. The Church insisted that all abortion is sinful and should be outlawed—even to save the life of the mother, even in the case of rape and incest.

With both the contraception and the abortion positions reaffirmed despite protest from many in the American Catholic Church, I—and many other Catholics—were faced with a Church whose teachings seemed increasingly out of step with our lives. Our all-wise Church, which had seemed so embracing, so understanding of human sin and weakness, did not seem so wise anymore.

I had enough Catholic education to believe that sex was not to be taken lightly. But I was not convinced that it had to wait till marriage. My readings in history had showed that throughout the Middle Ages—the height of the Church's power—couples were coupling well before a priest pronounced the marriage vows. I thought that sex made sense if I found the man I wanted to marry. We could learn if we were compatible. Luckily for me we were.

But life is not always so simple.

In 1974, I was a senior in college, and I wrote my thesis on abortion after one of my very good friends had gotten pregnant and, realizing that she did not have the wherewithal to raise a child, decided to have an abortion. It was tough for me to hear. This event hit me hard. I loved her. She was my pal—she was a good person and cared deeply about her family, helping her mother after her father had died, and was ready to devote much of her life's work to helping those least able to help themselves. I wanted to reconcile my love for my friend with the teachings of a Church that would condemn her as one of the world's worst sinners.

I undertook the project so I would have time to think of her, our friendship, and what our public policy should be. More important, I had heard from time to time growing up in the Church and from fellow Catholics that abortion was wrong. And after the *Roe* decision, the Church reaffirmed that position. But my friend's experience—the awful position she was in—made me look at the moral questions anew, and the reason for the Church's adamant, unforgiving, un-nuanced doctrine. It also made me realize that "pro-choice" was not the best slogan. I prefer "pro-conscience," for that clarifies that women make moral decisions.

The research was challenging. I was hoping to answer the question of how the Church had come to its position. Did it make sense? Was there a difference between a teaching of the Church and a law—the Commandments condemn swearing but nobody goes to prison for taking the name of God in vain. Most incredibly, how could the Church condemn abortion even to save the life of the mother?

To answer my questions, I looked at Church history and the history of the United States. Many of the books were almost impossible to find. I often had to go to medical libraries. They could not be checked out and had to be read under strict supervision. Because they were medical texts involving abortion, they were still censored. *Roe* had only just come down and the libraries were still adamant about what kind of information could be made public. I often needed special permission.

But what I learned was interesting. The Church had not always had such an unyielding anti-abortion stance. In fact, between the twelfth to eighteenth centuries, distinction was made between the "formed" and "unformed" fetus. As the twelfth-century canon lawyer Gratian stated, "He is not a murderer who brings about abortion before the soul is in the body." However, beginning in the mid-eighteenth century, the Vatican moved toward a much stricter stance, culminating in a very broad condemnation in 1930 in the encyclical *Casti Connubii*, in which Pope Pius XI refused to make any exceptions—even for the life of the mother. Austin O'Malley, the physician who wrote the definitive early-twentieth-century guide to Catholic medical ethics, *The Ethics of Medical Homicide and Mutilation*, taught that "therapeutic abortion . . . is never permissible under any circumstances." He insisted that if the choice is between mother and unborn child, the doctor must choose the child. "If the mother cannot be saved without emptying the uterus, the mother must die; there is no way out of the difficulty." At the end of my year of study, I took my first position against the views of my Church: I wrote that as a matter of public policy, the state should not punish women for what is the most difficult and personal decision.

That project, in a way, marked my loss of innocence toward my Church. Never in my youth had I seen Catholics stand up to their priests or to Vatican edicts the way I and so many other Catholics felt forced to do by the illogic and inhumanity of the Church's sexual declarations. Many in our community felt betrayed— betrayed by a Church that did want to recognize the changing needs of its flock. Women were working; extended families that might once have cared for myriad children were fraying. A large family may have made sense on the farm or if one had the resources my family was fortunate to have, but it made no sense to rule that contraception among married couples was sinful. And once there was this obvious crack in the Church's reasoning about a matter that was so central for women, for families, for children, the doubts about the

Church's wisdom only grew. The more one realized that the Church's dictates were coming from an all-male and technically celibate hierarchy that never had to worry about a mouth to feed or the joy of sex and its value for married couples, the more it seemed that this Church, while founded by God, was run by men who seemed more interested in their own traditions of power than in the needs of those they served. There was simply no way that Catholics could sustain the massive families that had once been the norm. And there was simply no way that Catholics who participated in the liberations of the feminist and sexual revolutions could adhere to the teachings of a Church that seemed so reactionary. The world was changing rapidly and the Church, which could engage in nuanced and detailed disquisitions on so many topics, such as it has done with the scholarship on "just war theory," could not do the same for women.

Still, I and many others did not leave the Church, though we could easily have found alternative denominations to welcome us. The Catholic Church is not something that you just join or leave as you would a country club or a business association. I had been baptized a Catholic, been confirmed as Soldier of Christ, had been imbued with Catholic teachings and Catholic culture. I had found solace in the fact that our Church had something irreplaceable and centuries old: a theology that helped me deal with tragedy, with sadness, sorrow, and the forces of evil. I loved its social justice tradition that flowed through our blood, as it had through my father's, and one that could not be drained so easily. Thirty years ago, the Church of César Chávez, the Berrigan brothers, Thomas Merton, nuns and priests, and wonderful activists was still going strong.

Throughout the Church's history, there has always been an uneasy balance between the Church that wanted to maintain its power and the one that used its prophetic voice to articulate the need for repentance and reform. At its best, embracing the latter, my faith demands that we examine our conscience, and care for the poor, sick, and less fortunate. It awakens within us the knowledge that we are fulfilled not through the mere accumulation of goods or power but by living for a greater purpose. "The spirit of our God is upon me: anointing me and sending me to bring glad tidings to the poor, to proclaim liberty to captives, recovery of sight to the blind and release to prisoners. To announce a year of favor from our God."

It gives us the sight to discern what is wrong, the hope that we can make things better, and the love to act with true compassion.

And so I love my Church. I appreciate its understanding of the spiritual community as a place where divinity actively dwells. The ritual of the Mass, the words of Scripture, knowledge that we can have time each week to pray and be connected to our past and to a spiritual presence are wonderfully enriching. I feel a mystical attachment to its traditions, to the saints who lived years ago, and to Catholics all around the world. As is written in Corinthians, "To each person the manifestation of the spirit is given for the common good." We are bound to one another, in spirit and in fact.

I follow in the path of other women who loved our Church—nuns, lay friends, strangers—and who are finding their inspiration from the stories of Jesus, Mary of Guadalupe, Our Lady at Lourdes, the Black Madonna in Kraków, the saints such as Joan of Arc, Teresa of Avila, Catherine of Siena. These foremothers enrich my life because I feel that we are part of the same tradition. They offer me the blessings and wisdom of a communion of saints. Jesus gave us a great example of staying within His tradition and still envisioning a new kind of community.

I believe that at the appropriate time the Church will reawaken to the promise of Vatican II. For even now, women and men are transforming our Church. They are speaking boldly for a vision of justice. They are finding new ways of reading Scripture, of understanding our history, of seeing God.

CHAPTER THREE

God's Work Must Truly Be Our Own:
The Catholic Church's Tradition of Social Justice

———∞∞∞———

Throughout my childhood, I felt enriched and inspired by my Church, its teachings, and its history. Through the stories of my grandparents, the example of my parents, and the education that I received from the nuns at Stone Ridge, I was brought into a warm and welcoming faith, and a Church that embraced the world and confronted evil in all its forms. No one was too young to learn this essential aspect of the Church's teaching. The sisters at Stone Ridge taught lessons of conscience and social action so that my classmates and I could carry forward our faith's tradition of justice, charity, and hope. At the earliest age, I learned that to be a good Catholic was to care about the condition of others, whether they were Catholic or not, and to sacrifice when needed so that the burdens of others could be eased.

If the obligations of Catholicism could be satisfied within the walls of the Church, our education would have been rather simple. Did we know the liturgy? Could we recite the catechism? How well did we know the lives of the saints? But that is only a small part of what it means to be a good Catholic. In school and in church, we were being prepared to take on God's work for ourselves, to improve—in a sense, complete—the world He created.

For a full century before my own birth, the Catholic Church was successful both at passing along these values to its parishioners and expressing them socially and politically. Impelled by Catholic social teaching and a growing immigrant community with needs both earthly and spiritual, the Catholic hierarchy played a leading role in nearly all of the reformist, progressive causes of the eighteenth, nineteenth, and twentieth centuries. The Church's record was by no means perfect. The Vatican was slow to condemn slavery and it was deeply ambivalent on women's political rights, not to mention our reproductive rights. The Church spent decades fighting to maintain laws that restricted the use of contraceptives, even by married couples. But its interest in sexual issues was overshadowed by the lessons of social justice. In its concern for the poor, for widows and orphans, for the sick, and for workers, the Church made the words of the Gospel come to life. And by preaching the Word of God in both word and deed, the Church was able to make American society more humane and just for everyone.

This is the Church that shaped me and the Church that I love. But I fear that it is in decline. In this chapter I want to recall the great tradition of social justice that characterized the Catholic Church in America for so many years and that must be reborn if the Church is to regain its role as a force for the betterment of humankind.

If I have an especially strong attachment to the Church's progressive traditions, it is because I know that none of my own or my family's good fortune could have been possible without it.

My ancestors arrived in America just around the time the Catholic Church was beginning to become a major force in American history. Thomas Fitzgerald, my great-great-grandfather, left Ireland during the potato famine of the 1840s, which killed a million people in Ireland and led to the emigration of two million more. Legend has it that Thomas's boat was headed to New York City, until a fierce storm blew the ship off course. One can only wonder how history might have been different had it not been for that storm. As it was, Thomas settled in the North End of Boston, one of the toughest and most crowded slums in any American city. When

Thomas's son, my great-grandfather John Fitzgerald, was born in 1863, the tenement in which he lived had one bathroom for twenty-four adults, thirteen children, and the customers of the bar on the first floor.

For my great-great-grandfather and his fellow immigrants, the Catholic Church was an anchor. It provided both a link to the Old Country and a network of support that helped them find work and assimilate into American life. Informal relief societies were established to manage the needs of parishioners, and the priests ensured that their congregations knew they had a responsibility to contribute. But the strongest bond was one of faith. It's hard to comprehend just how important religious belief was to early immigrants and how it guided their actions. For instance, just twelve hours after my great-grandfather was born, Thomas took the baby to St. Stephen's Church for baptism. At the time, many infants didn't survive their first few days and my great-great-grandfather apparently could not afford to take any risk that his own son would go to an early grave unbaptized.

Life for an Irish immigrant was perilous at every stage of life. Poverty, sickness, and death were ubiquitous in the Catholic slums. My great-grandmother, for instance, Josie Hannon Fitzgerald, whom my mother used to take me to visit many summer nights after dinner, suffered the loss of five siblings out of nine children before they reached middle age. Her experience was not unusual. The unbelievably crowded conditions were breeding grounds for disease. Tragedies were so common that there were many prayers for recovery— or repose of the soul if recovery did not come.

At the same time, Catholics could not feel welcome in the established government institutions. In Boston, schools and hospitals were dominated by the Protestant Brahmins. Catholic priests and nuns were not allowed in the city's hospitals and orphanages. The schools, too, were openly hostile to Catholics. Just a few years after my great-great-grandfather Thomas arrived in Boston, an anti-Catholic incident erupted in the very school Thomas's son, my great-grandfather, would attend a generation later. At the time, classrooms were overtly religious. Each day, students were made to recite the Protestant version of the Ten Commandments and the Lord's Prayer. When one Catholic boy refused, his teacher beat his hands with a stick until they bled. The other children said the beating lasted a half hour. The parents of the beaten boy sued and there was a trial, but the teacher was acquitted. The Boston establishment was unapologetic. One prominent Boston paper editorialized, "We are unalterably, sternly opposed to the encroachments of political and social Romanism, as well as to its wretched superstition, intolerance, bigotry and mean despotism—as much so as we are to the monster institution of human slavery and for the same reason." Several months after the trial, the Boston school committee ruled that Catholic children could no longer be forced to recite anything against their faith, but the story, and the anti-Catholic bitterness it evoked, was remembered long after.

Though they were brought up in privilege, my grandparents and parents were indelibly shaped by the prejudice Catholics felt when they arrived in our country. I grew up listening to my grandmother's stories of seeing "No Irish Need Apply" signs in shop windows, or reading bilious screeds against "Papists" in newspapers. As generous as America was to my family, the bitter memory of prejudice and the very real limits it placed on their lives provided a lens through which they viewed our country, and their role as Catholics within it. And through their upbringing, it shaped me, too. Even today, I can't pass by the Washington Monument without remembering a story I first heard as a child. In 1854, Pope Pius IX offered our government a gift of white marble from the Temple of Concord in Rome to be used in the construction of the monument. Shortly after construction began, members of the Know-Nothing Party, an anti-Catholic organization, stole the stone and it was never recovered. It's rumored to have been ground up and used as mortar. Congress, fearful of anti-Catholic prejudice, stopped funding the monument. Where it was finally restarted two decades later, the stone is of a different color. Whenever I pass by the monument, I think of my grandmother, her stories, and how dispiriting the vision of that monument must have been to immigrants trying desperately to belong in their new home.

Within the larger Catholic community, the experience reinforced a sense of identity and demonstrated the importance of sticking together, an attitude I saw reflected in my grandmother and her children. For new Catholic immigrants from Italy and Ireland, the grinding realities of poverty and prejudice meant that Catholics banded together and created their own community with its own institutions. Between 1877 and 1916, nearly 327 Catholic hospitals were founded, most of them under the management of nuns. By 1910, there were nearly 300 orphanages caring for more than 50,000 children. Catholic vocational schools were founded to help boys prepare themselves for the workforce. Shelters were founded for the homeless. And female religious orders, such as the Sisters of Charity, created homes for delinquent women, unwed mothers, abandoned children, and indigent elderly.

What amazes me most about the vibrancy of Catholic institutions during that time is the fact that the vast majority of Catholics were still so poor. And yet the size and scope of Catholic charity was unprecedented. In New Orleans alone, the historian Jay Dolan writes, "Catholics were supporting thirteen orphan asylums, an infant asylum, an industrial school for boys, a deaf-mute asylum, three homes for the aged poor, three hospitals, a home for newsboys, and a home for unwed mothers." The source of this incredible network was the collection plate that was passed around in church, from one hand to the next. However poor they may have been, they still knew that they shared a solemn obligation to give something back, whatever they could afford. Still today, we can see the legacy of that tradition. The Catholic Church still runs schools in the inner city, halfway houses for recovering addicts, hospitals, and homes for disabled and abused children.

As impressive as this network was, it was obvious to priest and layperson alike that charity could move the country only so far. If unfair labor laws consigned people to poverty, it wasn't enough merely to offer food to those who were hungry. You needed to change the law. If filthy streets and contaminated drinking water were causing entire neighborhoods to become sick, it wasn't enough to offer them free medical care. You needed to work with the city government to establish public health reforms. And if religious prejudice was preventing people from being able to find jobs, it wasn't enough to give the families of the unemployed a few dollars of relief aid. You needed to confront the problem at its source: the discrimination that contributed to the poverty of millions. This is a lesson I heard repeated in sermon after sermon, as, I imagine, did my parents and grandparents. It is the vital difference between charity and justice. The understanding that God has called us to pursue both at once represented the very heart of Catholic social teaching.

One of the landmarks of this teaching came just as my ancestors and their fellow immigrants were establishing themselves in our country. In 1891, Pope Leo XIII issued the revolutionary *Rerum Novarum* ("On the Condition of Labor"). The encyclical was very much a product of its time. Concerned about the growing popularity of socialism and communism, the Pope began by warning the faithful away from the godlessness and materialism at the core of these new economic philosophies. But in its attempt to balance economic freedom with economic justice, *Rerum Novarum* still resonates today:

> It is no easy matter to define the relative rights and mutual duties of the rich and of the poor, of capital and of labor. . . . [But] some opportune remedy must be found quickly for the misery and wretchedness pressing so unjustly on the majority of the working class. . . . Hence, by degrees it has come to pass that working men have been surrendered, isolated and helpless, to the hardheartedness of employers and the greed of unchecked competition. . . . [A] small number of very rich men have been able to lay upon the teeming masses of the laboring poor a yoke little better than that of slavery itself.

The encyclical was among the boldest and most far-reaching progressive statements in the history of the

Church and it reached a welcoming audience among American Catholics. Many were working in the mines, factories, and railroads. They, with their parish priests, nuns, and bishops, saw firsthand the destruction of family life, values, and health that such work could wreak. Its impact extended well beyond the clergy. Even non-Catholics were inspired by the message of the encyclical. The president of the American Federation of Labor delivered a lecture on *Rerum Novarum*, and activists across the country cited its teachings. Several years after its publication, a judge in St. Paul, Minnesota, refused to order an injunction against a plumbers' strike, using the Pope's words as justification. He explained, "If all the owners of capital and all the owners of labor would pay heed to the simple and beautiful lessons of justice taught in the encyclical from which I have quoted, there would be no labor troubles."

Rerum Novarum resonated beyond the Catholic community because it delivered a truly universal message. The intellectual and moral foundation wasn't purely scriptural. If it was, it would have necessarily excluded non-Catholics, or anyone who didn't accept the moral authority of the Church's interpretation of the Bible. No, the foundations were a clear-eyed view of the world and an understanding of the ethical obligation to help our fellow man. As a result, the message of *Rerum Novarum* was one on which Catholics and non-Catholics could find common ground. Here was the

Catholic Church working to unify all people under a universal set of ethical and political principles.

For me, this is the Church's truest self, Catholicism at its best. The world *catholic*, of course, means universal; in that sense *Rerum Novarum* was a profoundly catholic document. Whenever I begin to despair of the Church's recent retreat from the fight to create a just society, I remind myself of the moments when the Catholic Church lived up to its name, rose above the denominational limits, and spoke out on behalf of justice for all people.

This was the tradition out of which my family's political action grew. My great-grandfather was first elected to the Boston City Council promising to fight for his neighborhood. One of his first acts was to win funding for public playgrounds. The other councilmen—all from wealthy families—didn't see the point. They had land surrounding their homes where their children could play. But my great-grandfather remembered from his own life how hard it was to find a safe place to play. And he was also responding to his own understanding of his responsibility as a Catholic: to work, not merely for private gain but for the common good. I suppose because of the importance my great-grandfather placed on them, playgrounds have always symbolized something very precious for me and my family. So it was a special honor for all of us when the city of Boston named the park created by the Big Dig after my grand-mother.

My great-grandfather also cared deeply about the rights of immigrants, having witnessed how often they had been exploited and discriminated against. In 1897, he fiercely fought a literacy requirement for new immigrants. Today, my uncle Senator Ted Kennedy follows in the family and Catholic tradition and has stood up for the millions of new immigrants. Roger Michael Cardinal Mahoney of Los Angeles and Theodore Edgar Cardinal McCarrick of Washington, D.C., have also been adamant proponents of charity and justice for all immigrants.

In many ways, the early twentieth century was the first Golden Age of American Catholicism. Bishops and priests leapt at the chance to play a broader role in the community, and they were to some extent welcomed. Bishops such as John Spalding of Peoria, Illinois, were brought in to negotiate settlements of labor strikes. Spalding said the lesson of *Rerum Novarum* was that "the mission of the church is not only to save souls, but also to save society."

This spirit extended throughout the Church. Seminarians worked to create a theological basis for political action. The most influential was John Augustine Ryan's 1906 *A Living Wage: Its Ethical and Economic Aspects*, which the economist Richard Ely called "the first attempt in the English language to elaborate a Roman Catholic system of political economy." Ryan, a seminarian from Minnesota, soon became one of America's leading progressive voices and was instrumental in pushing American Catholics into political and social debates. In 1919, as hundreds of thousands of American servicemen were returning home after World War I had ended, Ryan was the lead author of the "U.S. Bishops' Program of Social Reconstruction." The report included calls for a minimum wage, government-run health and old age insurance, strict child labor laws, antitrust laws, and equal wages for women. "Its practical applications are, of course, subject to discussion," the report states, "but all its essential declarations are based upon the principles of charity and justice that have always been held and taught by the Catholic Church, while its practical proposals are merely an adaptation of those principles and that traditional teaching to the social and industrial conditions and needs of our own time." The American Catholic hierarchy was now front and center in the progressive effort to make America a freer, fairer, more just and humane nation for all its citizens, Catholic, Protestant, and Jew alike.

While most priests kept partisan political appeals out of their sermons, the connection between the religious obligation to help the poor and the political leaders who were fulfilling it was clear to any parishioner paying attention. In cities throughout the country, local politics were dominated by Irish Catholic political bosses. Some of them were corrupt, without a doubt, and city jobs and contracts were distributed on a spoils system, rather than on merit. But for these bosses to maintain their place in the community, they needed to make sure that the government took care of lower- and working-class Irish and Italian Catholics, who represented the majority of urban voters—at least in the Eastern cities—and the vast majority of the urban poor.

Catholic influence in national politics seemed to hit a wall in 1928, when Al Smith, the governor of New York known as the Happy Warrior, lost to Herbert Hoover in the presidential election. The 1920s were still roaring and concern for the poor wasn't a top political issue. At the same time Smith was the victim of one of the most vicious anti-Catholic campaigns in the history of our country. Historians looking back on the race say that an urban Democrat, Catholic or not, had little chance to win a national election. But for Catholics, the perception was that anti-Catholic bigotry kept Smith out of the White House. The anecdotal evidence wasn't hard to find, of course. The Ku Klux Klan, then a respectable political force in the South, spread all manner of vitriolic anti-Catholic campaign material. Hoover's refusal to disavow the material was even more stinging. The Republican Party seemed content to let the campaigns run their course, and states that had at that point traditionally gone to Democrats, such as Texas, Oklahoma, and Florida, found their way into Hoover's column.

It was a scarring experience for Catholics. After feeling welcomed in the early years of the century, the Smith campaign, or at least our understanding of it, came to symbolize just how far we had to go to be accepted. So deep-seated was the belief that when my uncle ran for president in 1960, even members of my own family were skeptical that the country was ready to elect a Catholic.

The Church could have turned inward and rejected a political system that, as we understood it, rejected us. But that's not the Catholic temperament, at least not the one in which I was raised. When the world seems to fall short of our expectations, Catholics move in to raise it up. Sure enough, when the Depression hit, the Church reinvigorated its position as a champion of justice. In 1931, Pope Pius XI released the encyclical *Quadragesimo Anno*, which took its name from the fortieth anniversary of Pope Leo XIII's *Rerum Novarum*. The encyclical reaffirmed the Church's support for workers and demanded that they have a role in the governance of the businesses in which they work.

It had an immediate impact in the United States and even normally conservative bishops acknowledged the need for reform. Cincinnati's Bishop John T. McNichols wrote that "one of the crimes of our country is the concentration of inconceivable wealth in the hands of a comparatively small group." Once again, the Church had tapped into its ability to speak across religious differences. One of the people inspired by the Pope's message was Franklin Roosevelt, who cited the document during his 1932 presidential campaign despite widespread anti-Catholic bigotry. At the risk of alienating a sizable portion of the country, Roosevelt called the encyclical "one of the greatest documents of modern times" and said it was "just as radical as I am." Catholics, even those such as my own family that had escaped the poverty of the urban ghettos, felt for the first time in years that the White House represented their values, too. It didn't hurt, of course, that Roosevelt appointed some very prominent Catholics to his administration—not the least of whom was my grandfather.

The Roosevelt presidency represented yet a new peak for Catholic influence. For many, it felt as though the New Deal vindicated the efforts the Church made in social action. There was a real sense of possibility for Catholics. This is when my grandfather began thinking that one of his sons could be president. The growing mood of acceptance was advanced by World War II, which, as many others have noted, helped smooth the divisions among American citizens. How could you hold on to prejudice against a Catholic or Jew or Southerner when you saw firsthand the bravery and patriotism of those different from you on a daily basis? Men from all backgrounds served alongside one another—Catholic, Protestant, and Jew, rich and poor. No one group was spared the inevitable tragedies. One of my uncles, Joseph P. Kennedy Jr., was killed piloting a plane. My uncle Jack was injured. My father served as a seaman first class. He often joked about how he didn't have the prestigious rank of his older brothers. But I think his jokes masked a certain pride in the fact that the power of his father, then the ambassador to the Court of St. James's—Great Britain—didn't spare him from any danger or confer any privilege. He started in the Navy as a humble seaman, just like so many others.

For Catholics, this meant an easing of some of the prejudices they had faced earlier. Suddenly, no one was questioning our patriotism or loyalty to country. My grandmother's memories made an impact, to be sure. But during my childhood, I can't imagine feeling a greater sense of belonging. Like so many other Catholic children, I grew up on a steady diet of movies that portrayed priests as the good guys. I remember Bing Crosby in *Going My Way*, Spencer Tracy in *Boys Town*, and Karl Malden in *On the Waterfront*. We were among the 30 million people who tuned in to Bishop Fulton Sheen's weekly TV program. His success took on a special importance among Catholics. The richness of the Catholic message seemed to have such universal appeal. We were on earth to do God's work—to fight for justice, to serve others, to maintain our integrity, to persist despite setbacks, to be resolute through troubled times.

Of course, the ultimate test of Catholics' greater acceptance within the country at large was John Kennedy's election as the first Catholic president of the United States. My uncle was not a deeply religious man. The deaths of his brother Joseph Jr. and his beloved sister Kathleen, after whom I'm named, left doubts in his mind that were never truly resolved. But it has always struck me as a sign of the power of the Church's role in the cause of social justice that his inaugural address was among the most overtly religious addresses since, perhaps, Lincoln's Second Inaugural. The speech mentions God three times: "I have sworn before you and Almighty God"; "the belief that the rights of man come not from the generosity of the state but from the hand of God"; and a paraphrase of St. Luke's admonition, pointing out that "Here on earth God's work must truly be our own," and quoting the prophet Isaiah's call to "undo the heavy burdens . . . and to let the oppressed go free." Moreover, the challenges he directed the nation toward represented in many ways the culmination of a hundred years of American Catholic development. Some of the lines read as though they came straight from *Rerum Novarum* or some other papal encyclical. America was to engage in "a struggle against the common enemies of man: tyranny, poverty, disease, and war itself." As if that wasn't Catholic enough, he quoted Romans, pledging that America would pursue this mission, "rejoicing in hope, patient in tribulation."

He spoke in a nonsectarian voice, but to us, it seemed an essentially Catholic message, one that we had heard thousands of times in our own Church services: We were connected to one another and the world. And just as our destiny was tied to the destiny of other peoples around the world, so, too, did we have a responsibility to ensure that justice and freedom—not the least being the freedom of worship—were available to all. The challenges he directed us to seemed to be the same ones the Old Testament prophets spoke of: poverty, illness, inequity. As such, there was something spiritually rousing about that time. He had excited our moral imagination with all the eloquence required when one is engaged in a tough and important mission.

And our Church responded. One of the things that make me proudest of my Church's history in this country is the fact that at the same time Catholics were the beneficiaries of greater tolerance, we also worked to extend tolerance to non-Catholics. The most important cause of justice in the second half of the twentieth century was civil rights, and it is a source of tremendous pride that here, too, the Church was an extraordinary force for good.

As proud as I am of the Church's history, the Catholic Church was not always strong on racial issues. The Vatican was slow to condemn slavery and Southern bishops often reflected the conventional prejudices of their communities. But for me, these seem to represent points at which the Church wasn't in touch with the universal aspects of Christianity and Catholicism. At its core, Christianity cuts against racial prejudice. Our identity isn't defined by our birth or our race, but our faith. We are all one in Christ. As the civil rights movement was beginning to get underway, many Northern congregations began to lay the foundations for the Church's role in the fights ahead. Long before the civil rights movement's first major victory of *Brown v. Board of Education* in 1954, Catholic dioceses were integrating parish schools. In 1939, New York City's Francis Cardinal Spellman announced that segregation had no place in Catholic schools. "There are no schools for Negroes. There are no schools for whites. There are only schools for all children."

After *Brown v. Board of Education*, the Catholic interest in civil rights grew, and the Church played a significant leading role through all the great battles of the 1960s. In 1958, the U.S. bishops set the tone by issuing "Discrimination and the Christian Conscience," which stated, "The heart of the race question is moral and religious." It didn't hurt Catholic involvement, of course, that the president who first made civil rights a priority was one of their own. But Catholic support for civil rights came from the very top of the Church hierarchy. In 1963, Pope John XXIII issued his own unequivocal statement of support for civil rights in the encyclical *Pacem in Terris*. "All men are equal in natural dignity," he wrote. "And so, on the doctrinal and theoretical level, at least, no form of approval is being given to racial discrimination. All this is of supreme significance for the formation of a human society." John XXIII's successor, Paul VI, deepened the Church's show of support by meeting with Martin Luther King Jr. in 1964. Support for civil rights ran throughout the Church hierarchy. "Church leaders preached racial justice from the pulpit," the historian Claire Wolfteich writes. "Priests escorted African-Americans into homes in white neighborhoods. Nuns in full habit marched down the streets of Harlem in solidarity with the Selma marchers. In Chicago five nuns and seven priests were arrested as they protested school segregation."

You can't overestimate the impact these steps had on Catholics. Obviously, I felt a special connection to the movement and its leaders because of my uncle's and father's close association with Dr. King. But for a young girl who, from time to time, entertained thoughts of joining a convent, the Church's acceptance of the goals of the civil rights movement made an undeniable impact. The vision of the Pope meeting with an African-American leader—a Baptist, no less!—was awe-inspiring. For us, the Church seemed to sanctify the movement and its leaders. Equal justice was no longer merely a political or legal issue. It was a moral issue, and central to what it meant to be Catholic. The role of Catholics was to oppose evil, and at that moment in time, the

Church made it clear in no uncertain terms that segregation was evil. And tolerating injustice, not merely perpetrating it, was a terrible sin.

The Church's unity on civil rights, sadly, was not reflected during the debate over the Vietnam War. The Church, like every other aspect of society, was split by the divisiveness of the war. Many leaders, including New York Cardinal Spellman, supported the war, as did many priests. In fact, I can remember becoming enraged during a sermon in which the priest criticized antiwar protesters. He insinuated that they had no right to question our government. At the time, I had never argued with a priest before, but I couldn't contain myself and after the service pointed out that Jesus Himself protested the actions of the Roman government under which He lived.

And, indeed, the antiwar movement was filled with prominent Catholics, including Father Philip Berrigan and his brother, Father Daniel Berrigan, my father, Dorothy Day, and Thomas Merton. But priests and nuns were among the most vocal protesters denouncing the war in Vietnam, even going so far in one case as to pour blood on draft files. Catholic lawyers and theologians, meanwhile, argued before the Supreme Court advocating for Catholic conscientious objectors.

The activism of the Church did in many instances lead to a backlash among conservative laity. One parishioner said, "this show of nuns and priests marching for this and that. . . . [W]e can accept the changes in the liturgy or theology, but these peacemakers stirring up trouble because of their conscience, God forbid."

Peacemakers stirring up trouble. Can you think of a better description of Jesus and the disciples? Can there be a better role for our Church leaders than to embody the values and attitudes that Christ and His followers did during their time on earth? The Church should be a source of spiritual comfort. But if all the Church provides is comfort, what good is it? The glory of the Church's history in our country is that it did not accept that the way things are is the way things should be. It constantly prodded its parishioners and its country to apply divine expectations to earthly problems. It's not always comfortable. But Jesus would not have us feel at ease while others suffer.

It is those moments when the Church seems to reflect that understanding that make me so proud. The Church helped to teach the importance of God's love, truthfulness, and compassion for those who suffer. And by embodying the idea that all people are equal in the eyes of God, it helped move our country closer to the dream of our Founders that all would be equal in the eyes of the law. My love for Church and country is never so great as when I realize that their aspirations for our nation and our world are one and the same.

CHAPTER FOUR

The Progressive Protestant Tradition

———— ⊶⊷ ————

I wasn't taught much about Protestantism as a child. Like a lot of American Catholics, my parents and grandparents felt ambivalent toward Protestant America, remembering the anti-Irish prejudice they and many others experienced. My grandmother Rose until the end of her life was pained by her memories of the Boston Brahmins who regarded Irish Catholics as "Popish, drunken louts." My grandfather left Boston for New York to escape the anti-Catholic prejudice that closed off many business opportunities to him. The only other image I had of Protestants as a young child came from the story of the Pilgrims whom we celebrated on Thanksgiving. Beyond that, the most I ever thought about Protestant America was to wonder if they could vote for a Catholic for president, and then, of course, to be grateful that they did.

My eyes, like those of so many others in so many ways, were opened by the civil rights movement and the religious character of its leadership and language. As I mentioned in the last chapter, I'm enormously proud that the Catholic Church lent its moral authority to the civil rights movement in America. But even as a young person I knew that Catholics weren't leading the way on this fight. It was a young Southern Baptist minister from Atlanta, Georgia.

During this momentous period in our history, I was privileged to have something of a front-row seat. I was nine in 1960, when my father and uncle interceded on behalf of Dr. King after he had been sentenced by a Georgia judge to six months' hard labor on a bogus traffic violation. My uncle called Mrs. King to offer comfort and solidarity. My father, after agonizing over whether helping King would cost his brother the Southern votes and ultimately the election, nonetheless called a Georgia judge and arranged to have King freed on bail the next day. Though there were real political risks, my father said he couldn't sleep "thinking about that Georgia judge putting a decent American in jail . . . because he was black and fighting for civil rights." Dr. King was skeptical of their motives and questioned whether it was just a politically convenient gesture. But his father, Dr. Martin Luther King Sr., was impressed. He said, "I had expected to vote against Senator Kennedy because of his religion. But now he can be my president, Catholic or whatever he is. . . . Because this man was willing to wipe the tears from my daughter-in-law's eyes, I've got a suitcase full of votes and I'm going to take them to Senator Kennedy and dump them on his lap."

In one sense, I remember feeling a real kinship with black people. My parents made a point to tell us that the children growing up under Jim Crow were just like us, with the same hopes and deserving of the same rights. But on a religious level, it was clear that there were real differences between the Southern black churches casting light on the injustice of segregation and the Catholic churches in which I was growing up. Priests got involved in political causes, but rarely could they act with the boldness and independence of Dr. King. While the hierarchy they represented gave them extraordinary influence, it also constrained their actions. A priest couldn't get too far out in front of the Church on any issue for fear of a rebuke from his bishop, or worse, from Rome.

But as far as Dr. King was concerned, he was answerable only to God. And he was unequivocal about how he recognized the path the Lord asked him to walk. In 1963, King was imprisoned for leading a peaceful protest. While he was in jail, eight white Southern clergymen wrote an open letter arguing that the proper place to address the injustices of segregation was the courts, not the streets. The fact that the letter came from clergymen represented a challenge to the religious character of the civil rights movement, but King was unyielding. If institutional churches and their leadership disappointed him, he wrote, he would "turn my faith to the inner spiritual church, the church within the church, as the true *ekklesia* and hope of the world."

This was a pretty radical idea for a young Catholic growing up before the Vatican II reforms. I was taught that the true Church didn't reside in our own hearts—it resided in Rome. The Pope was infallible. The rest of us were decidedly not. That's why we needed the Church hierarchy to teach us the right way to live and serve God. But for Dr. King, authority didn't reside within a hierarchy, or in tradition. It resided within his conscience, within his heart. His faith in the church within the church, in his ability to recognize and act on God's commandments, gave him the strength to withstand the overwhelming violence that was brought down on him and those who marched with him.

Many liberals today look upon Martin Luther King Jr. and the civil rights movement as an aberration within American history: a time when the Protestant faith played a decisive role in the cause of justice. But the civil rights movement represented more of a continuation than an exception. King and the ranks of ministers he inspired and led were drawing on a centuries-old tradition of Protestant faith and public action. The reason,

I believe, that Dr. King left such a lasting impact on the soul of our country is because his words and actions brought life to ideals that have been at the heart of our country, and the faith of Protestant Americans, since the days of the first settlers. The voice of faithful Protestants has been heard at each of those moments when our nation moved closer to its promise of equal justice for all—the American Revolution, abolition, the New Deal, and the civil rights movement, and more.

Of course, this isn't the religious tradition in which I was raised. But the ideas at the heart of Protestantism with all its incredible diversity are so deeply rooted in our political culture that it's in many ways difficult to separate them. And so even though it isn't my faith, it has indelibly shaped the political tradition that has shaped me and that I care so much about. Protestant or not, this tradition is a part of me, too, as it is every American.

Regrettably, the influence of Protestant churches on our nation's politics today appears almost uniformly conservative. Not unlike those of the Catholic Church, the leaders of Protestant congregations have come to disregard the New Testament's teachings on charity and justice and have instead tightly focused their outrage on issues of sex and private conduct. Of course, these issues aren't new to Protestant churches, especially evangelical congregations. But the narrowness of the Protestant community, this moral myopia, is a break from our history and a betrayal of the proud Protestant tradition of progressivism. In a day when Protestant churches in particular are associated with a conservative turn in our country, these traditions and the way they shaped our history need to be recovered from memory, celebrated for the good they accomplished, and reestablished as the heart of modern Protestantism.

Because I know how deeply my own faith has shaped my political beliefs, I've always been interested in how the faith of others has influenced their own ideas and actions. The civil rights movement was not the beginning of the progressive tradition within Protestantism. Far from it. But it did represent one of the most profound flowerings of the ideas and themes that drove Protestant involvement in progressive causes and reform movements for hundreds of years in our country.

What are these ideas? I believe there are three specific Protestant beliefs that have driven progressive and reform-minded causes throughout American history. First, the legitimacy of protest created the conditions necessary for revolution, all the while establishing an example for future reform movements. Second, the spiritual equality of all individuals created a model for political equality, and set in motion the series of rights movements that continue to expand the circle of freedom in America. Finally, the notion that, as the creation of God, we have the potential to perfect ourselves, and the society in which we live, has been essential to driving people toward greater justice.

The roots of this tradition extend back to the first Pilgrim and Puritan settlements. I can still remember my mother taking my brothers, sisters, and me to Plymouth Plantation as a child. It was important to her that we learn the history of the country that had given us so much opportunity. We were taught to admire the colonists' courage and fortitude and to acknowledge our debt to them. But like most Americans of the time, I was taught that the Puritans were a bit priggish— moral scolds who were obsessed, as the old saying went, that someone, somewhere might be having fun. They came to America, in a sense, to escape modernity and create a righteous, theocratic community.

Only later, in college, did I learn how much the progressive tradition owes to the first colonies. The Puritans were not looking to retreat from the world. They were looking to fulfill it. Their mission, as John Winthrop declared in his sermon aboard the *Arbella*, was to build a "New Jerusalem," an example to the world of the truth of God's word. "For we must consider that we shall be as a city on a hill. The eyes of all people are upon us," Winthrop reminded his fellow colonists, so it was incumbent upon them to model the faithful Christian life.

When in college I first studied the history of the Puritan colonies, I remember being struck by how extroverted their vision was. I always associate a concern for the common good with Catholicism. But Winthrop's language was familiar to me. Indeed, it was much the same language as those of the Hebrew prophets. The sins the Puritans sought to purify the church of were selfishness, greed, and neglect of the less fortunate. On board the *Arbella*, sailing toward the New World, Winthrop told the settlers that they would be bound by the law of God's love. What did this mean in practice? "First," he said, "that every man afford his help to another in every want or distress. . . . We are commanded this day to love the Lord our God, and to love one another. We must delight in each other, make others' conditions our own, rejoice together, mourn together, labor and suffer together."

If the sense of shared responsibility seemed familiar to me, their belief in their own authority was certainly not. Indeed, the most profound contribution of the Puritans to progressivism was to establish, in word and deed, the notion of the legitimacy of protest. Indeed, they brought it on the boat with them when they left England to escape the persecution of the Anglican Church.

The concept of protest is so central to Protestantism that it's in the very name. And indeed the idea is so deeply ingrained in our culture that it's hard to see how radical it was. But considering they came to our country at a time when church and state were one, when rebellion against the king meant rebellion against God, the real courage of the Puritans becomes clear. The

English king at the time, James I, understood this rather well. "No Bishop," he once said, "no king." Indeed Americans would eventually prove him right, and the Puritans took the first step. One of the leaders of the new Puritan colony was utterly matter-of-fact when he was confronted by an Anglican bishop. "We conceive a different apprehension of the mind of Christ" than you and proceed "as in the spirit we are bound to follow the Lamb whithersoever he goeth and after the apostles example, as we believe, so we speake." Three hundred fifty years later, Dr. King uttered the same sentiment, and in a way, it was still radical.

But the political genius of Protestantism was not simply the freeing of individual conscience, critical though that is, but the mobilization of those who disagree with powers and principalities. Protestantism did not create hermits. It unleashed powerful energies in search of a public good. The Puritan movement, in many ways for the first time in history, created a model for collective organization, activity, opposition, and reform. The philosopher Michael Walzer credits them with creating the notion of "the organization of zealous men for sustained political activity," the idea that "organized bands of men might play a created part in the political world." Protest became the essence of what it meant to be American, and Americanism was the essence of political protest. As Edmund Burke put it in 1775, the American patriots constituted "the dissidence of dis-

sent and the Protestantism of the Protestant religion."
Moral protest, a principle that brought life to progressive movements for hundreds of years, was, through
the faith of the Puritans, the bedrock of our national
character. Once a believer defines for himself what
God wants, politics is utterly transformed. The authority of king, bishop, governor, or police chief is irrelevant in the face of one's understanding of divine
will.

If Winthrop and the Puritans seeded America with
the tradition of protest, it was George Whitefield, Jonathan Edwards, and what is now known as the First
Great Awakening that established the principle of equality to America. This, too, was a revelation for me. I had
always been taught, like a lot of Americans, that the democratic freedoms came directly from Enlightenment-era
deists like Ben Franklin and Thomas Jefferson, who
looked for inspiration not in the life of Jesus but further
back to the example of ancient Greece. Without belittling the matchless genius of the Founding Fathers and
the centrality of humanism to their beliefs, this vision of
history papers over the revolutionary power that faith
had at the dawn of our country.

Edwards, Whitefield, and the other preachers of the
Great Awakening were active in the middle part of the
eighteenth century. Edwards was from Northampton,
Massachusetts. Whitefield was an English preacher who
came to America at first to raise money for an orphanage,

later to spread the Gospel. Each would go from town to town holding revivals, drawing Americans out of their churches and into open-air meetings that could last for days. Both were known as fiery preachers and, like the Puritans, were mostly remembered for their fire-and-brimstone sermons. (Edwards's most famous sermon bears the decidedly illiberal title "Sinners in the Hands of an Angry God.") But the sermons of the eighteenth-century evangelists contained a great deal of hope and love as well. Most significant, historically, Edwards suggested the radical idea that the gates of heaven were open to all, each of us was a child of God and carried within a spark of the divine, full members within a "priesthood of believers." Within us was the power to choose to move toward God, or to stay apart from Him.

Those in power recognized the threat this posed to their authority. The British secretary of state at the time said of Whitefield's theology that "Every man being thus allowed to be his own Pope, he becomes disposed to wish to become his own King." He wasn't far off. In a sense, Edwards and Whitefield led a movement to democratize religion. And a democratized faith established the foundations of a democratic culture. If God spoke through men, then the voice of the people was, in a sense, the voice of God. If that was so, then the only legitimate government would be one that was steered by the democratic means. "What we now see in America, and especially New England," wrote Edwards in 1742, "may prove the dawn of a glorious day . . . so often foretold in Scripture." God is using America, Edwards preached, for the "moral and political emancipation of the world." The colonists believed that they were part of something noble and important. Their vision was enlarged. Their hearts were filled with the courage to undertake great tasks.

Faith overpowered all the old boundaries: geography, class, even race. Poor and rich alike were welcome at revivals and told they had an equal share of God's love and salvation. Up through the early nineteenth century, white and black evangelical preachers shared the same pulpit, preaching to mixed congregations, even in the South. White audiences recognized the radical message at the heart of the evangelists, and history has preserved the testimonies of many white Christians admiring the powerful prayers of black worshippers. A white Methodist from Mississippi, for example, wrote of listening to the prayers of a black slave at a revival meeting. "The earth seemed to tremble under the weight of that power . . . the whole audience seemed to sway to and fro . . . cries for mercy, groans of agony, and shouts of praise were so numerous and loud that, strong and loud as his voice was, one could scarcely hear him." And black Americans at the time, the majority of whom lived as slaves, felt the liberating power of the preachers' message. Phillis Wheatley, a black poet living in Massachusetts, eulogized Whitefield in her first public poem. Assuming the voice of the great preacher, she wrote, "Take him, ye Africans," she wrote. "He longs for you, Impartial Saviour is his title due."

Nearly a hundred years after Edwards and White-field ignited the Great Awakening, the theology behind the movement developed into the heart of the abolition movement. Faithful Protestants soon became the leaders of the movement, perhaps the first significant cause to rally progressive people of faith to commit themselves to social and political action. Although Southern churchgoers marshaled Scripture verses that they deemed "pro-slavery" in defense of their position, religious progressives were united in their belief that slavery was an unchristian activity. In so doing, they rejected the biblical passages cited by slave sympathizers that showed slavery existing in biblical times and instead chose to emphasize the biblical message that each person is made in the likeness of God. It was a triumph of love over literalism.

The ranks of abolitionists were filled with white Protestants from the North down to the Mid-Atlantic who agitated for emancipation for slaves. One of these crusaders was Theodore Parker, a Unitarian minister who rooted his anti-slavery views in biblical precedent: "The arc of the universe is long, but it bends towards justice," he preached. The idea that God resides not in the institution of the church or the authority of the clergy, but inside people themselves, meant that everyone—slave included—was part of God's community. It's hard to overstate how revolutionary this belief was and its impact on progressive churches and individuals. Good Christians simply could not allow their brothers and sisters in Christ to be kept as slaves.

It's a testament to the power of this idea, and the hold it had over the hearts of Americans, that it enabled us not only to fight the Civil War but to recover from it. Today, even the political divisiveness of an election seems too entrenched to overcome easily. How much more difficult, then, must it have been to stitch together a nation after a war that lasted four years and took the lives of more than 600,000 countrymen? But the notion of spiritual equality extended not only to slaves, of course, but to Southern slaveholders as well. It rings throughout Lincoln's Second Inaugural Address, in which the president extended a sainted hand of brotherhood to the Southern half of the nation. Both North and South, he said, "read the same Bible and pray to the same God, and each invokes His aid against the other. . . . With malice toward none, with charity for all, with firmness in the right as God gives us to see the right, let us strive on to finish the work we are in, to bind up the nation's wounds, to care for him who shall have borne the battle and for his widow and his orphan, to do all which may achieve and cherish a just and lasting peace among ourselves and with all nations."

If there's one thing history teaches us, it's that freedom, once unleashed, refuses to respect traditional boundaries. Just as Protestantism opened the door to see the humanity of black slaves, so, too, did it enable some to recognize the potential of women. In some ways, this was more controversial within the Protestant community than even the issue of slavery. Progressive Protestants took egalitarianism to its logical ends, but more conservative forces, who believed in the inerrancy of the Bible, could not overlook the many verses that called on women to be subservient to men. We're still seeing the legacy of this battle today in the opposition of some evangelical organizations to the women's movement.

But the Protestant community was the first component of society to offer real positions of leadership and responsibility to women. Women preached. Oberlin College, which was founded by the evangelist Charles Finney, began granting degrees in theology to women. Women adapted the language of rights, freedom, and equality to their own struggle. They honed their political skills first in the fight for the freedom of slaves—and then in support of their own liberation. Lucretia Mott, a Quaker lecturer, and Elizabeth Cady Stanton got their start in politics as abolitionists, and soon included women's rights in their mission after they were denied full participation at a London conference. They organized the Seneca Falls Convention in 1848, announcing in their creed that "the Creator has endowed men and women with inalienable rights." Stanton even produced a women's version of the Bible to counteract conservatives who cited Bible verses to oppose her movement. Abby Kelley Foster, another abolitionist, put it succinctly: "We have good cause to be grateful to the slave. In striving to strike his chains off, we found, most surely, that we were manacled ourselves."

The final, and perhaps most influential, Protestant innovation began to take hold in the nineteenth century, during what was called the Second Great Awakening. This was the idea that human beings have it within their power to perfect themselves, and ultimately society. Few stated it with more beauty than Ralph Waldo Emerson. In an 1841 lecture, he said, "The power, which is at once spring and regulator in all efforts of reform, is the conviction that there is an infinite worthiness in man which will appear at the call of worth, and that all particular reforms are the removing of some impediment. Is it not the highest duty that man should be honored in us?" The progressive Protestant ethic became that of removing the impediments that kept us from fulfilling our God-given potential of perfection.

I can't deny at the outset that this notion has had negative repercussions. Anytime religion extends itself into the political realm, there's a real threat that the usual disagreements will escalate. It's one thing to disagree with someone's political objectives. It's quite another to disagree with the way they believe God wants society to operate. Opposition quickly becomes viewed as heresy, and there is no greater threat to a pluralistic society. The fact that perfectionism was taking hold around the same time as the massive wave of Irish and Italian immigration probably contributed a great deal to the anti-Catholic prejudice that my grandparents and great-grandparents encountered throughout their lives. The effort to create public schools, for instance, was helped immeasurably by Protestants who believed the schools would "cleanse" the minds of young immigrant Catholics of their old-world faith.

But at the same, I can't ignore the extraordinary impact the notion of perfectionism had on our country. Protestant reformers believed that the New Jerusalem Winthrop spoke of was within reach. God's kingdom on earth was no longer just a prayer: It was a practicable goal to be realized through politics. No longer could Christians tolerate poverty or suffering of any kind. Protestant reformers such as Dorothea Dix, who cast attention on the degraded conditions of prisons and mental asylums, took seriously Jesus' example of extending kindness to the outcast. Hospitals, orphanages, and homes for single mothers were founded, and what was perceived as the causes of social problems, such as drinking, were attacked with missionary zeal.

The belief began to have a real impact toward the end of the century. Ministers throughout the country,

Northern liberal and Southern evangelical alike, became part of what became known as the Social Gospel movement, so named for its efforts to apply the lessons of the Gospel—injunctions to feed the poor, care for the sick, clothe the naked—to contemporary social and, later, political conditions. A bestselling book, Charles Sheldon's 1896 *In His Steps*, introduced the phrase "What would Jesus do?"—still popular today—and prodded Christians to walk in Jesus' shoes by decrying and addressing the poverty around them. The proponents of the Social Gospel were very much in the minority in the last half of the nineteenth century, but as the unpleasant side effects of industrialization became more apparent, their message began to resonate more deeply with working-class Americans and others who sympathized with their troubles.

This new breed of reforming preacher spoke truth to power, and helped to shape the agenda for change: child labor laws, women's suffrage, the forty-hour workweek, the recognition of unions, laws mandating safe working conditions, and a livable family wage were all advanced by progressive efforts. Organized efforts of Protestants created the Salvation Army and YMCA to address the problems of urban poverty. Protestants also copied Catholic efforts to establish hospitals. Years later, Franklin Roosevelt, while more of a political realist than a Social Gospel proponent, nonetheless described the New Deal to a group of ministers as an effort to enact the Sermon on the Mount. The Great Depression had overwhelmed the efforts of volunteer agencies. But the ethic of service and progressivism had completely infused the work of the government.

Of course, the apex of this tradition came just a few decades later, when the twenty-six-year-old Dr. King agreed to support a boycott of Birmingham buses. Liberals especially look back on the civil rights movement as something of an aberration in American history, a time when religion and progressivism worked together to make our country more just, fair, and equal. Not long ago, in fact, I attended a conference on religion and politics at a progressive think tank. Each of the speakers spoke on the example of Dr. King. But there was no mention of Winthrop, or Whitefield and Edwards, or Emerson. To them, it seemed as though the history of progressive Protestant faith began and, sadly, ended with Dr. King.

Perhaps there is more at work here than just short memories. The triumph and martyrdom of Dr. King mask the real opposition he faced from secular forces within the liberal establishment who believed that his religious rhetoric would be alienating to key components of the liberal coalition, especially Catholics and Jews. Liberal suspicion of religion is no less pronounced today, and as a result, those moments in our history when Protestantism served as the moral ballast of progressive causes are downplayed.

This makes it all the more important to recognize that Dr. King continued a tradition, rather than created it. If we look back on the civil rights movement, all the major themes of Protestant progressivism are clear to the eye. We can see Winthrop's faith and courage in the actions of those marchers who defied Bull Connor's attack dogs and fire hoses. We can hear Edwards's and Whitefield's belief in each person's equal share of divinity in Thurgood Marshall's arguments against the injustice of segregated schools. And we can feel Emerson's faith in the infinite worthiness of man and society in Dr. King's dream of an America that "lives out the true meaning of its creed: 'We hold these truths to be self-evident: that all men are created equal.'" No one ever expressed such a clear and compelling vision of a perfect America as King, when he looked ahead to the time when "every valley shall be exalted, every hill and mountain shall be made low, the rough places will be made plain, and the crooked places will be made straight, and the glory of the Lord shall be revealed, and all flesh shall see it together."

The Protestant faith in America has sought to guide America to the Promised Land since John Winthrop and the passengers of the *Arbella* disembarked in Salem, Massachusetts, in July 1630. Even if Dr. King didn't invent this legacy, he reminded us of its power. In doing so they helped to unite the faith community in the cause of justice. White and black, Christian and Jew,

Catholic and Protestant alike were marching together in the streets in protest, in hope, and in faith.

Ultimately, the Protestant faith has been a force for inclusion in America, one that widened the circle of friends and followers and redefined positively what it meant to be an American. Those who I believe have most aptly imitated Christ's admonition to love our enemies reached out to those with whom they disagreed. King exemplified this. He wanted to eliminate his enemies not by harming them but by persuading them to join his cause. Each reminds us that to be religious can entail an opening of the heart, a humility about one's own righteousness, and a yearning to broaden the city, the country, the priesthood of believers.

The aberration from our history is not found in the 1960s, but in the decades that have followed, decades in which the American Protestant leadership has all but severed its connection to its proud tradition of progress.

CHAPTER FIVE

What Does It Mean to Be a Christian Nation?

———— ✺ ————

Newsweek called it the "Year of the Evangelicals." In the midst of a presidential election year, polls showed that an unprecedented number of American voters professed a faith in the inerrancy of the Bible and claimed to have been "born again." While the history of evangelical Christianity stretches back to the time of the American Revolution, never before had evangelicals played such a decisive role on the national political scene. In addition to influencing countless local, state, and congressional races, the votes of Christians propelled to the White House America's first evangelical president. For the first time in our history, the nation elected a president who spoke openly of the importance of his personal relationship to Jesus and the centrality of that relationship to his political leadership.

The year? 1976. The president? Jimmy Carter.

In thirty years, the influence of religion on politics has been turned entirely upside down. Whereas in Carter's election, evangelicals were considered something of a swing vote, today they are the largest, most loyal, and most conservative part of the Republican Party's base. In 2000, President George W. Bush received 68 percent of the evangelical Christian vote. Four years later, his support among white evangelicals was even stronger, at 78 percent.

As we saw in the previous chapter, Protestants played a defining role in the most vital progressive movements in our country's history, from the birth of the American democracy to abolition to civil rights. No more. Mainline Protestant churches are in decline and have to a large extent retreated from political discourse. Meanwhile, evangelical churches have grown larger and more politically assertive, putting a decisively conservative stamp on our nation's politics. While individual evangelicals have been found to hold far more nuanced political positions than most people think, evangelical political leaders have moved the private issues of sexuality and reproduction to the forefront of the nation's discourse. Meanwhile, the belief that we have a shared responsibility to ease the burdens of the poor and less fortunate has been all but abandoned.

Don't get me wrong. There's no question that evangelical churches have helped millions of Americans turn their lives around and endure the inevitable tragedies of life. I've seen the incredible role the churches play in the lives of many of my friends. Privately, evangelical churches have been an extraordinary force for good. But the rise of right-wing evangelicalism and the force it has exerted in electing ever more conservative politicians has served to undermine the sense of national unity and collective responsibility that has mattered so much throughout American history.

This wasn't inevitable. There's nothing intrinsic to evangelicalism that dictates a commitment to lower taxes and more lax environmental standards. Far from it! Indeed, there's a growing chorus of progressive evangelicals who are more than capable of pointing out the ever-widening distance between the Gospels and the Republican Party platform. But for the moment, they are a minority within the enormous and enormously influential right-wing Christian community. As a whole, there can be no question that the American Protestant community has dropped its commitment to social justice, dealing a terrible blow to our country's efforts to come to the aid of the people and families the Bible demands we help.

In this chapter, I will discuss how the Christian Right came to be and show how much more there is to being a Christian nation than they believe.

Churchgoing Americans are more likely to vote—and more likely to vote Republican—than nonchurchgoing Americans. And the more religious you are—the more you attend church—the more likely this is. And in America, there's no group more tied to the church—for worship, companionship, and political direction—than the evangelical communities. On a full range of issues, from the economy to social issues to the question of national security, evangelicals are even further to the right than the average Republican, much less mainstream Americans. And because conservatives have spent so much time and effort mobilizing these churches for political campaigns, they have become an extraordinarily powerful political force. "The advantage we have," Ralph Reed, the former executive director of the Christian Coalition, has said, "is that liberals and feminists don't generally go to church. They don't gather in one place three days before the election."

How did evangelicals grow into such a politically potent force?

To a large extent, the power of the Christian Right today is the culmination of a three-decade-long reaction to the social justice movements of the 1960s.

After the fever-pitched battles of civil rights and the Vietnam War, a lot of churchgoers were looking for a return to normalcy. Rather than turning to their pastors and churches for an inspiration to political action, they were looking for a haven *from* political action. In one 1969 study, researchers found that 77 percent of Protestants and 68 percent of Catholics (but only 43 percent of Jews) agreed that they "would be upset if my (minister/priest/rabbi) were to participate in a picket line or demonstration."

Civil rights proved to be a particularly divisive issue for some congregations. Some of the first signs were seen as far back as the early 1950s, when many white Southerners began creating "Christian academies," private schools to send their children to so that they would not have to learn in desegregated classrooms. I can't help but think how utterly unchristian the genesis of the "Christian academies" truly was. The retreat from the public schools was only accelerated by Supreme Court decisions in the early 1960s prohibiting state-mandated religious ceremonies and prayer in school.

As the civil rights movement pushed forward in the 1960s, the backlash became even more intense. President Lyndon Johnson is said to have remarked after the passage of the Civil Rights Act, "There goes the South for a generation." He was more right than he knew. Forty years on, there's been no shaking Republican control of the Southern states.

It wasn't just in the South. The clergy's role in the civil rights movement proved difficult for churches all across the country. In 1969, sociologist Jeffrey K. Hadden wrote:

In the New York Episcopal Diocese, one layman withdrew a $600,000 pledge because of his opposition to the clergymen's involvement in Civil Rights. In the same diocese a similar financial sum was lost in pledges to the building fund of the Cathedral of St. John the Divine. Bishop Horace W. B. Donegan admitted that the Cathedral's position on racial justice, including the hiring of a Negro priest, was the major cause for the withdrawal of pledges. . . . [B]ut the Episcopal Church is not alone in this conflict. . . . In a Washington suburb, the assignment of a Negro minister to an all-white Methodist congregation brought a 50 percent decline in attendance and a similar reduction in financial contributions, in spite of the fact that the pulpit committee had voted unanimously to accept a minister "regardless of race."

Many ministers were concerned that their parishioners' dissatisfaction with their political advocacy would lead to the breakup of their congregations. As one minister said of the prayer-based protests at the time, "Each of us has some fine noble laymen who love the Lord, neighbor, and church, and who feel keenly that 'kneel-ins' are no part of Christianity." One researcher found that many liberal clergymen "feel that for the time being the church should pay more attention to its traditionalist functions and to healing the wounds left by the activist sixties."

For many Americans, the inward turn took yet another step: one toward evangelical Christianity and its shift of focus from earthly justice to individual spirituality. "Southerners," the progressive Southern evangelist Tony Campolo once told me, "did not like the Bible telling you to like black people, so the right wing wanted a church that simply talked about a right relationship with Christ." One study of baby boomers found that more than one-third of those who grew up in mainline Protestant churches left, with half of those moving to conservative congregations. Many complained that their previous churches didn't answer their spiritual questions and longings.

They had a point. The theological reasoning that led to an activist clergy had been established so long ago, many pastors no longer realized they had to keep explaining the connection between the Gospels, justice, and an individual's relationship to God. The lessons I learned in Catholic school and from sermons about how service moves us closer to God got lost. Political action was never supposed to be a substitute for a relationship with God, but a means to it. But few heard those words coming from the pulpit. So politics became seen as something superfluous to the core mission of a church, rather than what it was, and is: a public expression of God's commandment to work for justice.

The vacuum created an incredible opportunity for

conservatives. They made the most of the opportunity to bring this growing constituency into their camp. Conservative political activists met with evangelical leaders to discuss ways they could solidify evangelical support by advancing divisive social issues, such as opposition to abortion and gay rights, that would force evangelicals otherwise concerned with issues of social justice and economic fairness to align with the right.

For the past two decades, Republican politics has been geared toward solidifying support among white Christians. As a result, Republicans have been able to count on solid support from the evangelical vote. Most of this has been because of the deft exploitation of what have become known as "values" issues. Despite their role in advancing conservative economic policies, the Christian Right has organized itself in opposition to abortion, gay rights, the teaching of evolution, and the women's movement. At first, these were grassroots uprisings in protest of local school district decisions or state ballot initiatives. Today, they are well-orchestrated national political campaigns devised in Washington and promulgated thanks to a billion-dollar conservative Christian media infrastructure.

The problem with the Religious Right's focus on so-called values questions is that it has the effect of making our faith seem undemanding. Nowhere in the Gospels does Jesus suggest that His followers should be content with their own righteousness and be judgmental of others. If the Gospels teach us anything, it is that we must be forgiving of others while always expecting more of ourselves: more sacrifice, more compassion, more love for our neighbor. And yet the leaders of the Christian Right have made Christianity seem effortless because they sermonize most often and most intensely on the sins their congregations for the most part can avoid. It's always someone else who's doing the sinning—Hollywood, homosexuals, the Darwinists, the feminists—and so the judgments can come tumbling down fast and furious. It's always someone else who is responsible for the moral breakdown of society. But when it comes to the hard stuff, the stuff that demands that all of us give of ourselves to better the lives of those around us, the right-wing preachers are nowhere to be found. It's as if they believe that Jesus healed the sick, fed the hungry, and cared for the poor just so we don't have to.

Jesus cautions us to judge not. If there is a central message to Christianity, if there is an enduring lesson to the example Jesus set during His time on earth, it is that none of us is without sin. None of us is perfect. When one follower called him "Good teacher," Jesus responded, "Why do you call me good? No one is good but God alone." What an extraordinary challenge to His followers. If even Jesus expected more of Himself, how can we not apply the same moral introspection to our own lives? Jesus didn't give up His life to make it easier for us to damn those who are different from us. He gave His life so that we could learn how to redeem our own. And He lays out precisely how we are supposed to do that: by serving those around us.

Here is where I believe modern evangelical leaders stray so far from the Gospels. Conservative Christians are fervent supporters of the anti-tax, anti-environment, pro-corporate policies of the libertarian wing of the Republican Party. But it isn't that they are lending religious credibility to causes and issues about which Jesus says nothing. Rather, they always seem to be working directly against Jesus' explicit instructions. In Mark, a rich man approaches Jesus and asks Him, "What must I do to inherit eternal life?" Christ doesn't mince words: "Go, sell what you have and give to the poor, and you will have treasure in heaven. Come, follow me."

Over the past generation, the country's wealth has become increasingly concentrated within the richest families at the top. In the past thirty years, for instance, the percentage of American wealth owned by the richest 1 percent of the country increased from 22 percent to 40 percent. And yet for the past few years, the Christian Coalition has made its top legislative priority "Making permanent President Bush's 2001 federal tax cut." They seemed unconcerned that these tax cuts would provide a windfall to the wealthy and thereby make it much harder for them to "squeeze through the eye of the needle" into heaven.

There's something deeply troubling and inconsistent about evangelical support for conservative economic policies. Essentially, they've chosen to abandon any notion of shared responsibility and the idea, well supported by both the Hebrew prophets and Jesus Himself, that we have an obligation to improve the world, an idea that was central to both Catholic and Protestant political traditions throughout our history. Indeed, Christian conservatives admit as much. In March 2005, decrying the renewed efforts of a few evangelicals to help the poor and become better stewards of God's creation through environmental action, the conservative columnist Cal Thomas wrote a column that seemed to sum up the conservative attitude: "There is no biblical expectation," he wrote, "that a 'fallen' world can, should, or will be improved prior to the return of the One to whom evangelicals are supposed to owe their complete allegiance. . . . Jesus is appropriated these days for all sorts of things with which he would have nothing to do."

Thomas, I should say, distinguishes himself from many on the Religious Right by saying that Christians shouldn't be focused on any politics, left or right, but on spiritual conversion. But even so, he's reading the Scriptures rather selectively, and a growing majority of evangelicals seems to agree with the interpretation. Increasingly, "health and wealth" Christianity, and the politics it spawns, has become accepted as gospel. Rather than believing that Jesus asks us to serve and sacrifice for the sake of one another, Christians seem to think that so long as we say and feel the right things, it doesn't matter if we *do* the right thing. But as it says in the hymn "Lead On, O King Eternal," "For not with swords' loud clashing, nor roll of stirring drums; with *deeds* of love and mercy, the heavenly kingdom comes."

Deeds of love and mercy are few and far between among some luminaries of the Christian conservative movement. In a 2004 *Newsweek* profile of Tim LaHaye, the co-author of the *Left Behind* series (which has sold 62 million copies worldwide), the reporter asked LaHaye how he reconciles his luscious lifestyle (as he describes his home, "this beautiful place, and that drop-dead gorgeous view of the mountains" in Rancho Mirage, California) "with Jesus' injunction to sell all you have and give to the poor." LaHaye responded, "I can accomplish far more from my present lifestyle and the giving that I do to Christian work. If I just sold everything and gave it to the poor, I can't see where that would advance the Gospel as much as I'm doing." "But wouldn't it advance the poor?" the reporter asked. "Well," LaHaye replied, "you know how much I pay in taxes?" And yet, said Jesus, "Do not lay up for yourselves treasures on earth, where moth and rust consume and where thieves break in and steal, but lay up for yourselves treasures in heaven, where neither moth nor rust consume and where thieves do not break in and steal. For where your treasure is, there will your heart be also."

I am somewhat sympathetic to the conservative complaint that throwing money at the problem does not always solve it. There were certainly some misjudgments in the War on Poverty. But the difficulty of a task is no excuse for giving up. My father would always quote Marcus Aurelius, who said, "Prefer the hard." And there is lots of evidence that public action can have real positive effects on the missions Jesus called us to. Food stamps have reduced the number of starving children, the Earned Income Tax Credit has helped stabilize families—as have the increase in child care subsidies and family leave benefits. Social Security has raised the elderly from the poorest demographic group to a much more financially secure position—and one that is healthier, too. When Jesus says, "For you always have the poor with you," He was not giving His followers carte blanche to ignore their needs. Conservatives often interpret this verse to mean just that, conveniently ignoring the thousands of other verses in the Bible enjoining us to commit ourselves to charity and mercy. So when faced with the shortcomings of, say, health care, the Christian position should be, "If this isn't working, let's find something that does." The

Religious Right, however, says, "This isn't working, so let's do nothing."

Many times, it seems the source of their indifference to poverty is hostility toward the poor. Whether or not one agrees with the efficacy of public action to combat poverty, one cannot dispute our religious and moral obligation to try to better the lives of the less fortunate. More important, in fact, we must love them, seeing in the face of all humanity the image of Christ.

But so many leaders of the Christian Right seem to regard the poor with naked contempt, denying their worthiness of compassion as well as our obligation to come to their aid. Pat Robertson, who has built an empire worth hundreds of millions as founder of the Christian Broadcast Network, once responded to the idea of health care for the poor by saying, "You are guaranteed the poor will be stealing from it like they do food stamps and everything else." Arguing against welfare, he said of single mothers, "If you want to pay them five hundred, six hundred, seven hundred, eight hundred dollars a month, or whatever it is, to have a baby, they'll have babies. And if they'll stop paying them, they'll stop having babies. It's that simple." His words simply ooze with contempt and hatred. I can't think of anything more unchristian.

Indeed, the hostility is all too often expressed not only in words but in deeds, mostly through conservative political activism and lobbying. In 2003, Alabama's

Republican governor Bob Riley proposed new taxes to help fund the state's public school system. There was no question of the need. That year, Alabama fourth- and eighth-graders scored lower than any other state in the nation on reading and math tests. And yet Alabama, despite the high percentage of its citizens who identify themselves as Christians, rejected the new taxes by a two-to-one margin. Leading the way was the Alabama Christian Coalition. The chapter's president, John Giles, explained, "You'll find most Alabamians have got a charitable heart. They just don't want it coming out of their pockets." I have never heard a more twisted definition of "charity." What could it possibly mean to have a charitable heart if your hands are clutching your wallet?

Indeed, inasmuch as the new evangelicalism seems concerned with doing good, its focus is entirely on "what's good for me." The Christian Booksellers Association list of bestsellers is filled with self-help books that suggest Jesus cares mostly about your physical comfort. In earlier years, religious authors used spiritual language to call for Christian involvement in the cause of social justice, in books like Walter Rauschenbusch's *Christianity and the Social Crisis* and Reinhold Niebuhr's *Moral Man and Immoral Society*. To be sure, these weren't written for a general audience, but their message infused the language of preacher and politician alike. Today, evangelical literature seems entirely concerned with how faith in God can make you happier, healthier, even wealthier! For all intents and purposes, Janis Joplin's lyrics are being sung without a hint of irony. People do want the Lord to buy them a Mercedes-Benz, and authors are getting rich telling their readers that He will.

Sometimes the simplistic narcissism and crass materialism of these books is comical. But modern evangelicalism's selfish individualism has taken a heavy toll on our politics. Whether the cause was war or poverty, whenever sacrifice has been called for, the American people have been able to summon the ability to give of themselves for the greater good of our nation. The Christian faith of Americans has been a deep well from which our nation could draw in times of trouble. It was true in the Civil War, in both world wars, and during the Depression. But when a growing number of Americans no longer believe that their faith impels them to serve others or to sacrifice any degree of personal comfort or security, our country will no longer be able to count on that elemental and vital aspect of citizenship.

I think we can see signs of this all around us. It can be seen in our shortage of teachers and nurses and police officers. And while trust in the military is at record levels, recruiters are having a hard time meeting their quotas. No doubt, the deep national divisions brought about by the Iraq War have played a major role here.

But consider that there is near consensus that the men and women in our military are our greatest heroes on whom our security and liberty depend.

Why, then, can so few Americans seem to summon the will to be a hero for our country? Why can so few find the spirit of service within them to volunteer and give their efforts for the sake of others? It's not Americans' faith that's lacking. More Americans claim to be religious and attend church more regularly than at any point in decades. But when religious leaders say that God wants us most of all to be comfortable, it undermines our ability as a nation to achieve the feats of selflessness that our country demands during times of trouble.

When Jesus was asked what was the essence of God's Law, He replied, "You shall love the Lord your God with all your heart, and with all your soul, and with all your mind. This is the great and first commandment. And a second is like it. You shall love your neighbor as yourself. On these two commandments depend all the law and the prophets."

Bill McKibben, writing in *Harper's Magazine*, correctly noted that "American churches, by and large, have done a pretty good job of loving the neighbor in the next pew. . . . But if the theology makes it harder to love the neighbor a little farther away—particularly the poor and the weak—then it's a problem. And the dominant theologies of the moment do just that. They undercut Jesus, muffle his hard words, deaden his call, and in the end silence him."

But there is even more at stake than politics. Looking back at Jesus' answer to the Pharisee, I'm struck by how He makes a point of saying that the second commandment is "like" the first. The two are not merely parallel, but interwoven and interdependent. To love our neighbor is to love the God in whose image he was created. To love our neighbor is to love the Spirit of God that suffuses him. Likewise, to deny our obligation to love our neighbor, no matter how different from us he or she may seem, is to deny our obligation to love God. Indeed, it is to deny God Himself, because we are denying the spark of divinity that imbues every person, binding us to one another and to our Creator.

Jesus puts no limits on how we are to show our love. He makes it clear: with all our heart, with all our soul, with all our mind. It means we can't look at the poor with cold eyes of contempt. It means it isn't enough to have a charitable heart; we must have charitable hands. And it means that when we are considering how to fulfill our obligation of charity, we must look for the ways in which we can have the greatest effect on the lives of those we seek to help.

"Love," says Corinthians, "is patient and kind; love is not jealous or boastful; it is not arrogant or rude. . . .

Love bears all things, believes all things, hopes all things, endures all things; love never ends."

This is the spirit I find lacking in the words and actions of today's Christian Right and, consequently, in our country.

CHAPTER SIX

Misbegotten Males and Other Misconceptions:

Where the Catholic Church Went Wrong

—— ∞∞∞ ——

As I showed in the previous chapter, American Protestant churches began to retreat from their progressive traditions due in part to their congregations' reaction to the divisive battles of the 1960s, especially that of the civil rights movement. Their abandonment of the Social Gospel created a void of spiritual leadership that might have been supplied by the Catholic Church. But it didn't happen. After reaching a high point in the 1980s, the Catholic Church, like its Protestant counterparts, began to turn away from its own progressive tradition. But the Catholic Church's conservative turn didn't involve the issue of race. Instead, it came about in reaction to the women's movement.

Over the past forty years, Catholic women like me

have sought to play a more influential role in the Church, just as they have in the secular world. The Catholic hierarchy might have seen this as an opportunity to renew the Church by opening its leadership to the half of the Catholic community that had always been excluded. Instead, I believe it saw women's desire to participate within the Church's leadership as a threat to its own power. As a result, the Church took hard-line positions on women's issues and elevated their importance above all aspects of the Church's teaching, leading the Church to take a sharp turn away from its traditions of social justice.

The severity of the Church's response has been devastating. In addition to alienating a growing number of Catholics, the Church's retrenchment on women's issues has overshadowed the importance of the Social Gospel and the good it can accomplish in the world. By focusing so intensely on women's issues, the Church has in effect alienated those of us who care about the Church's expansive teachings regarding the importance of charity and justice. As a result, the Church has done terrible harm to Catholic unity, undermined its own moral credibility, and endangered its future.

In this chapter I hope to show how the Catholic Church abandoned its core teachings, the damage this has caused, and why I believe it can—and must— choose a different path.

*   *   *

During the past 150 years, the Catholic Church has spoken up on myriad issues—labor rights, immigration, health care, housing, gun control, the Cold War, the minimum wage, maternal leave, contraception, the death penalty, and more. While the Church more often found itself on the side of progressives, rarely did it abide by the simple political distinctions of left and right, Democrat and Republican. On many issues, such as the Cold War and women's rights, the Church was more in line with the conservative elements of American society. The Church's independence served it well. No party could take the Church's support for granted, and few doubted the integrity of the Church's word in political matters.

No more. Increasingly during the past thirty years, the Church hierarchy has placed the issue of abortion above all others.

I've seen this firsthand throughout my career in public life. My own pastor criticized me from the pulpit for my opinion on abortion when I was running for Congress in 1986. But it continued even after I left office. In 2003, I was asked to speak at the graduation of my old school, Stone Ridge, in Bethesda, Maryland. After it was announced that I would be speaking, demonstrators, almost none of them affiliated with the school in any way, began to protest. The organizer told the local papers that I was "a poor choice for graduation at a Catholic school because her policies differ so much from Church teachings." I was saddened that their view of the Church's teachings was so narrow. Yes, I disagreed with the Church on abortion rights. On the other hand, I always believed that much of my work was deeply informed by my Catholic upbringing and the lessons I learned at Stone Ridge. The idea that each soul was precious, that every person was indispensable in the sight of God, stood at the heart of everything I tried to do—from the effort to get kids involved in community service to providing health care for everyone. But to the protesters, there was only one issue, one litmus test for Catholics: abortion. And I was on the wrong side.

I'm not the only politician targeted by conservative Catholics. Far from it. In 1984, then Archbishop John O'Connor said he would consider excommunicating New York governor Mario Cuomo because while he was personally opposed to abortion, Cuomo refused to push for government restrictions on women's reproductive rights. During Mary Landrieu's campaign for Senate in 1996, the archbishop of New Orleans, Philip Hannan, told parishioners that if "a person actually believes in Catholic doctrine, then I don't see how they can vote for Landrieu without a feeling of sin." And in 2002, Archbishop Michael Sheehan approved of priests throughout the state of New Mexico distributing flyers criticizing gubernatorial candidate Bill Richardson's position on abortion. (I should mention that each of these candidates won reelection.)

While these controversies simmered in different spots around the country throughout the 1980s and 1990s, the issue took on national importance in the presidential election of 2004. Early that year Archbishop Raymond Burke announced that he would deny Communion to Senator John Kerry, a former altar boy, because of Kerry's support for legal abortion. While some bishops around the country publicly disagreed, notably Theodore Edgar Cardinal McCarrick of Washington, D.C., Joseph Cardinal Ratzinger, now Pope Benedict XVI, sent a letter to American bishops. The letter was not an official statement of Vatican policy, but since Ratzinger was prefect of the Congregation for the Doctrine of the Faith, the overseer of official Church doctrine, it carried plenty of weight. The letter did not mention Kerry by name, but Cardinal Ratzinger said that Communion should be denied in "the case of a Catholic politician consistently campaigning and voting for permissive abortion and euthanasia laws." Going even further, Ratzinger wrote that anyone who votes for a pro-choice candidate is "guilty of formal cooperation with evil" and therefore "unworthy to present himself for Holy Communion." If the cardinal's wishes were carried out, about 20 million American Catholics would have been effectively excommunicated from the Church.

Despite differences with the Church's teaching on war, poverty, the death penalty, gun control, and more, never has a conservative politician been threatened with being denied Communion because of his or her position. But the Church's single-mindedness doesn't end even there. Despite saying that every abortion is a murder, the Church has never expressed concern over the fact that the number of abortions under Republican administrations has been significantly higher than that under Democratic administrations. Because their absolutist position on abortion seems to drown out every other issue the Catholic Church purports to care about, it has the effect of making all of those issues—including the goal of reducing abortions—seem unimportant. Their actions suggest that they prefer ideological purity over effective action.

Politics, it's often said, makes for strange bedfellows. But as a Catholic and someone who's had more than a passing interest in politics, I would hope that the Church would aspire to something more transcendent than electoral politics. Otherwise, it becomes little more than just another interest group, and one that is betraying the Gospels, to boot. When I visited Sandra Schneiders, a nun and professor of theology at the Jesuit School of Theology at Berkeley, she asked simply, "Where in the Scriptures do we find anything about abortion? But I can find throughout the New Testament, 'Love your enemies, do good to those who persecute you. Pray for those who hurt you. When someone strikes on one cheek, turn the other.' How often should you forgive? Not seven times seven, but seven times seventy times. And they are telling you to ignore this."

Dr. Schneiders's question points to the reason even anti-abortion Catholics should be troubled by the Church's direction. The Church is undercutting its own moral authority and influence. No Catholic, liberal or conservative, should want their Church to be thought of in such degraded terms.

But we can't change the Church until we recognize how it came to this point in the first place. How has this issue become the alpha and omega of the modern Church?

As Dr. Schneiders suggested, the answer is not found in Scripture. Nowhere is the question of when life begins considered in the Bible. As I showed in Chapter 2, the issue has been debated over time and the Church has not been consistent. It wasn't until the nineteenth and more so in the twentieth century that the Church took its now familiar hard line against all abortions, even those to protect the life of the mother. Moreover, at no point has the Church ever believed that full funeral rites are appropriate for fetuses that miscarry, a fate that meets anywhere from 15 percent to 50 percent of all pregnancies. And even when the Church did establish a clear position against all abortions, it recognized that, when making political choices, it had to be considered as one issue among many.

What happened? The women's movement happened.

As the women's movement began to make progress throughout secular society, Catholic women, including nuns, began to look at the Church with new eyes. Here was an institution where the authority of the hierarchy had been unquestionable, and that hierarchy was exclusively male. Women's voices rarely, if ever, could affect Church doctrine. When in the early 1960s the Second Vatican Council was being planned, the Vatican polled bishops, as well as heads of men's orders, for ideas regarding what issues to discuss. The heads of women's orders were not consulted. No women were asked to participate in the council's first session in 1962. Only after Leo Joseph Cardinal Suenens of Brussels remarked that "half of the Church" was missing from the discussion were women invited to join. A few women were included in subsequent discussions, but they were not allowed to vote. All together, fifteen women participated in Vatican II, next to nearly three thousand men.

The Church simply was not prepared to adapt to the heightened aspirations of modern women. Women, and the question of their rights and responsibilities, have been tricky for the Church since its beginning. Theologians, time and time again, emphasized the particular and unique sinfulness of women. Augustine argued that only men, not women, were made in the image of God. St. Thomas Aquinas defined women as "misbegotten males."

The misogynistic strain of Church thinking found

roots in America as well. Church leaders were early opponents of women's rights, especially suffrage. And when a rare priest dared to argue that women should be able to cast a vote, it wasn't out of a belief in the importance of women's voice to democracy. One prominent Boston priest argued in favor of suffrage not because it would empower women, but because it would empower priests! Surely, he argued, Catholic women would obey the political guidance of their pastors "with edifying docility and zeal."

And so when Catholic women started to ask questions about their status within the Church, the hierarchy was ill-equipped to respond. And how could they not be? What experience did a group of celibate men have with the particular experiences and challenges that women face? Presumably, they could have recognized the limits of their experience and reached out to the women of the church. But as the pederasty scandal demonstrated, the Church hierarchy, when confronted with a choice between serving their flock or protecting themselves and their authority, choose themselves. On the issue of women, once again, the male hierarchy chose to assert the absoluteness of their authority.

Starting in the 1980s, for instance, the United States Conference of Catholic Bishops tried to develop a pastoral letter on women's issues, such as they had done on peace and the economy. But after nine years, in 1992, the process broke down and nothing was produced. The bishops wanted to emphasize issues that American women endorsed, such as the need for equal pay and child care. The Vatican vetoed that approach, insisting that the letter contain disquisitions on contraception, abortion, and the priesthood.

But it wasn't just disagreement on the issues that wrecked the discussions, it was the nature of the process itself. The bishops refused to believe that they had anything to learn from listening to women. The late Bishop P. Francis Murphy revealed that the very act of consultation was the issue that raised the most concern about the pastoral letter among the bishops. The bishops, Murphy said, "asserted that Bishops are teachers, not learners; truth cannot emerge through consultation."

When I think about this kind of attitude, I take solace from the example of St. Catherine of Siena, and I marvel at her bravery. St. Catherine was the fourteenth-century mystic and political activist who helped negotiate peace among the papal states. Her greatest achievement was to convince the Pope to return from his exile in Avignon and restore the papacy to Rome. "This is His will, father," she told the Pope. "This is what he is asking of you. . . . Since he has given you authority and you have accepted it, you ought to be using the power and strength that is yours. If you don't intend to use it, it would be better and more to God's honor and the good of your soul to resign." The Pope abided. She is remembered, some joke, because it's the last time the Church ever listened to a woman.

In the twentieth century, whenever women have had the chance to demand change from the Vatican, the story has been different. Confronted with the very real and legitimate complaints of women, the Church chose to retrench and dig in its heels to resist reform.

It shouldn't be a surprise. In a lot of ways, the Church is no different from any other large institution. It can be slow to adapt to change. It's reluctant to admit its own errors. And the people within the hierarchy jealously guard their own power, often mistaking their own interests with those of the people they are supposed to serve. And because of the religious nature of their authority, the Church can always invoke its religious authority to shield itself from criticism. What might be unmasked as errors within a more democratic organization can be enshrined into unassailable canon law, and persist for centuries. There's a saying that comes from a sermon of St. Augustine: *Roma locuta, causa finita*. Translation: Rome has spoken. The issue is settled.

That may have worked in the fourth century. But in the past forty years, Rome's judgment has been the beginning of the debate, not the end.

The debate over contraception is an ideal case in point.

Like abortion, the Church's position on contraception has changed throughout the centuries. Church leaders preached that procreation was the one and only legitimate purpose of sex. In the twentieth century, this position softened a bit. But sex was still supposed to be primarily for the sake of procreation and any artificial means that a couple took to stand in the way of the will of God was a sin.

For a time it appeared as though the Church might change its position. In 1962 Cardinal Montini, the future Pope Paul VI, put together the Papal Birth Control Commission to make recommendations on whether or not the Church should change its position on birth control, and what effect that might have on papal authority. The commission included sixty-four laypeople and fifteen clerics, including a Polish archbishop named Karol Wojtyla, who of course would go on to become Pope John Paul II. After a four-year process, the committee decided that while declaring birth control permissible would in the short term undermine Church authority, the Vatican should nonetheless do so, because it was simply the right thing to do. According to newspaper reports at the time, the laypeople on the commission voted 60 to 4 for the change, while the clerics voted 9 to 6.

But the Church is not a democracy and Pope Paul VI considered the judgments of both the majority and the minority. Karol Wojtyla (now a cardinal) wrote on behalf of those against the change. "If it should be declared that contraception is not evil in itself," the cardinal wrote, "then we should have to concede frankly that the Holy Spirit had been on the side of the Protestant churches. . . . It should likewise have to be admitted that for a half century the Spirit failed to protect Pius XI, Pius XII, and a large part of the Catholic hierarchy from a very serious error."

In other words, we can't change our mind without admitting that our predecessors were wrong. And if they were wrong, then what does that say about our own claim to divine authority?

The Pope was swayed by the argument that if the Vatican admitted to having been wrong, the entire foundation of the Vatican's power would be shaken. It was too big a step for him to take. In 1968, the Vatican released the encyclical *Humanae Vitae*, reaffirming the Church's ban on artificial contraception.

The knowledge that the Church was more interested in seeming right than being right contributed to the firestorm set off by *Humanae Vitae*. The Church's authority was deeply hurt by the fact that it appeared to care more about its tradition than the men and women of God that they were currently serving. And so couples simply began ignoring Church teaching. The percentage of Catholic couples that used birth control increased from 30 percent in 1955 to nearly 90 percent today. Catholics who got used to disregarding this teaching soon became adept at discounting others as well. In *A*

People Adrift, Peter Steinfels quotes a priest who claims that in his thirty years as a priest, no married couple had ever once asked about the Church's teachings on contraception. The word of the Vatican on the issue was simply irrelevant. While the Church hierarchy was figuring out the best way to preserve its power and authority, the laity decided to get on with their lives and walked right on by.

The Church's eagerness to protect its power expressed itself in the battle over women in the priesthood as well.

The Vatican has gone to great lengths to prevent women from fully realizing their gifts, both spiritual and intellectual, within the hierarchy of the Church. In 1979, during Pope John Paul II's first visit to the United States, Sister Theresa Kane, who was at the time head of the Sisters of Mercy and president of the Leadership Conference of Women Religious, had what became a famous encounter with the Pope. She greeted the Pope with the request that the "Church in its struggle to be faithful to its call for reverence and dignity for all persons must respond by providing the possibility of women as persons being included in all ministries of our Church." Basically, she was asking the Pope to reconsider his decision to prohibit all discussion of female priesthood. The crowd—as well as countless Catholics such as myself around the country—applauded her boldness, but the Vatican was not amused. After the

Pope returned to Rome, the Vatican asked Sister Theresa to reconsider her views and tried to intimidate her into rescinding her statement. She's a hero to many today because she did not.

Many more nuns and women in the laity have told me that the experience of Mercy Sister Sharon Euart was just as chilling. In 2000, Euart, a canon lawyer who had been the associate general secretary for the U.S. bishops' conference, was prohibited by the Vatican from assuming the general secretary position. The official reasoning was that she was not a priest and that it was not the "custom" around the world. In fact, both South Africa and Scandinavia had had lay general secretaries. But apparently Rome did not want a woman in the United States because of its prominence. There was no argument about her competency, just her gender. To add insult to injury, the new general secretary forced her to resign her position as an associate. As a result, there were no longer any high-level women in the U.S. bishop's conference, in spite of a 1994 promise by the bishops to bring women into more top-level Church positions.

How does the Vatican defend its position?

First, the Church says that the exclusive ordination of men reflects Jesus' will. Since He chose only men as apostles, that suggests that He meant for only men to be in the priesthood. There's a certain absurdity to this argument, though. Jesus also restricted His choice of apostles, as Steinfels writes, "to circumcised Palestinian Jews." Indeed, Jesus seemed to make several radical overtures to defend the spiritual standing of women. Whenever I've been troubled by statements by Church leaders that suggest women have second-class spiritual status when it came to our relationship to Jesus, I've always comforted myself by recalling the story of Martha and Mary. When Martha complains that Mary is sitting at Jesus' feet listening to His preaching rather than helping her to prepare the meal and clean up, Jesus says that Mary is doing "the better part." For those of us who have been sweeping, mopping, washing, drying, dusting, taking out the garbage, sorting socks while someone else had the pleasure of simply talking, laughing, hanging with friends or other interesting people, Martha's complaints certainly seem justified. But, seen in the context of the time, it is liberating: Women were not supposed to be learned or wise about theology. And yet here is Christ blessing a woman's attempt to be just that. This welcoming attitude toward women, in fact, is reflected throughout the Gospels. In light of Christ's openness to women's spirituality, is it so difficult to recognize that He would accept women in the priesthood today?

Second, the Church says that, since the role of the priest is to represent Christ to his ministry, it is necessary that the congregation be able to see the face of Jesus in the face of their priest. If a woman said the

Mass, the Church declared in a 1976 encyclical on women in the priesthood, "it would be difficult to see in the minister the image of Christ." No doubt this would take some imagination. But would it take any more imagination than a belief in a virgin birth or resurrection of Christ? If, during the Eucharist, a cup of wine and a wafer can become the very blood and flesh of Jesus, why can't a woman embody the spirit of the Savior? In fact, people seem quite able to make just this leap of faith. Today, more than 60 percent of American Catholics believe women should have the opportunity to be priests. The laity, not surprisingly, is far ahead of the hierarchy. Americans are saying that they can indeed see the face of Christ in that of woman. How can the Church, then, argue that we can't?

The Church is left with one last, familiar argument. Tradition. Just as it said in arguing for maintaining the prohibition against contraception, the Vatican argues that since the priesthood has always been restricted to men, changing would shake the foundations of the Church's authority.

This is absurd. The idea that the Church can't change its mind because earlier Popes could not have been wrong suggests that the Church has never, ever changed its mind about anything. And yet, for centuries the Church held that Jews bore a moral stain for the killing of Christ, before it decided in 1965 that they did not. The Church stood by and refused to call slavery a

sin until 1888, when Pope Leo XIII issued a weak condemnation of slavery in Brazil. Usury has been considered a sin since the first days of the Church, but that has
not stopped the Vatican from having interests in the
banking industry. It took over 350 years before the
Church reversed itself and rescinded its condemnation
of Galileo for refusing to recant his belief that the earth
revolved around the sun. Less than two hundred years
ago, one Pope called railroads the "work of the devil."
And for centuries, Catholics were told that the souls of
unbaptized babies would spend eternity in Limbo. Yet
in 2005, the Church declared that this was no longer
part of Catholic cosmology. If the Holy Spirit didn't prevent past Popes from making these errors, then who is
to say that today's Popes and cardinals could not be in
error in their understanding of women's issues? Is it so
great a stretch of the imagination to believe that previous Popes and theologians were merely blinded by the
limits of their own culture? God is infallible, but people
are not. Can we not revere the traditions of our Church,
all the while understanding that the men who shaped
those traditions may have been creatures of their own
time? There is no sin in that. But there is sin in holding
fast to prejudices when time has revealed their error. If
the Church can admit that it was wrong about slavery,
and astronomy, and trains, why can't it say the same
about women?

This brings me back to the question of abortion.

Obviously, I don't believe that anti-abortion Catholics feel the way they do merely to protect the power of the Church hierarchy. Abortion is a deeply complicated and difficult issue and I would like to believe that good people, even good Catholics, can disagree.

But when, on the two other major women's issues, the Church relies on an argument that seems to prove nothing but the hierarchy's interest in preserving its power, one has to wonder. I do believe that many Catholics' concern for the lives of the unborn is sincere. But at its core, the hard line that the Church takes against supporters of abortion rights seems to come back to the question of its power. The issue of abortion is simply too high profile for the Church to brook dissent. If it concedes that it may be wrong, that its word is not the absolute reflection of the will of God, their authority vanishes.

But they're wrong. By appearing out of touch with the lives of their flock, by refusing to consider the voices of lay Catholics, they endanger the very thing they are trying so hard to protect. As with the issue of contraception, with which the abortion debate has so many parallels, Catholics may start to get used to ignoring the Church. That's when the Vatican's hierarchy truly collapses.

Indeed, we're already beginning to see signs. The Church's missteps on women's issues, and its subsequent conservatism, are alienating women and threatening the long-term health of the Catholic Church.

A recent survey by James Davidson produced for a conference on "The Church in America" held at the Wharton School found that young women were much less satisfied with the Church than men because of issues such as abortion, birth control, and women's ordination. Many women I've spoken to have complained of feeling shut out of the Church, but few have put it as succinctly as Kiri Cardegna, a former nun who left the Church after hearing one too many sermons belittling the contributions and potential of women. When I visited her at St. Agnes Mercy Theological Center in Baltimore, she told me, "I no longer wanted to be part of an institution which had no place for me. . . . I wasn't going to waste my energy trying to change an institution that was so huge, so steeped in patriarchy."

There is a certain cognitive dissonance that a woman feels when she walks into her church. Out in the secular world, we can achieve positions of leadership and responsibility. The old prejudices about what roles a woman can and can't hold are falling away. More than three-quarters of the country have said that they'd be willing to vote for a woman for president, and given the steadily increasing number of women holding seats in Congress and statehouses around the country, there's no reason not to believe them.

But within the walls of the Church, we are viewed

no differently from the way our great-grandmothers were. Whatever we may have accomplished in the secular world, in the eyes of the Church, a woman's identity is primarily that of a mother and a nurturer. Now, I'm proud to be a mother, and even prouder of the four daughters my husband and I have raised. But motherhood isn't the sum total of my identity. Just as African-Americans would resent participating in an institution where segregation was still considered legitimate, so, too, do women I've spoken to resent the expectations the Church imposes on us. The Church is supposed to be the home of timeless truths. But today, walking into a Catholic church is like walking back in time.

For all the good Pope John Paul II did in speaking out against communism and oppression throughout the world, I'm afraid he did very little to improve the standing of women in the church, which, in terms of the Church's governance, was a more essential and enduring challenge. Shortly after his election in 1978, the Pope began a process within the Vatican to reaffirm the Church's views on women's role in the world and the Church. The result, delivered more than a decade later, were two Apostolic Letters titled *Redemptoris Mater*, "On the Blessed Virgin Mary," and *Mulieris Dignitatem*, "On the Dignity and Vocation of Women." Pope John Paul II certainly made some important first steps. In *Redemptoris Mater* and *Mulieris Dignitatem* the Pope did acknowledge and regret the Church's misogynistic history. He broke with the long tradition in which women were considered sinful, less than men, and the "devil's gateway," and reasserted the primacy of Genesis, where women, like men, are made in the likeness of God.

But even so, the Pope's image of a woman's role is constricting and, therefore, not fully equal. According to Pope John Paul II, a woman's "personally feminine" vocation has two particular dimensions: virginity and motherhood. "In the light of Mary," *Redemptoris Mater* argued, "the Church sees in the face of women the reflection of a beauty which mirrors the loftiest sentiments of which the human heart is capable: the self-offering totality of love, the strength that is capable of bearing the greatest sorrows; limitless fidelity and tireless devotion to work; the ability to combine penetrating intuition with words of support and encouragement."

Don't get me wrong. I love Our Lady and have four statues of her in my bedroom and one in my study. But the Pope's portrayal of women rested on caricature. Yes, I would like to be kind, giving, intuitive, and supportive. And being a mother is part of my identity, but it is not the sole sum of who I am. But the Pope omitted the fact that even for women who do bear children, more than half our lives are spent in roles outside that of reproduction and parenting. Sure, women have love and devotion to offer. But we also have reason and vision and ability. (Just as men have the capacity for support and compassion.)

I hope that Pope Benedict XVI thinks anew about what it means to be made in the image and likeness of God and follows the course of the logic. For it is the very idea that we are made in God's image that gives the Church its transcendent power. Our faith should draw from that essential aspect of our soul that is pure spirit. If the Church starts from this point, rather than from an attempt to justify its long history of misogyny, it has a much greater chance to reach out to women and renew our Church for the next century and beyond.

The Church is called to act. No other institution has the resources to offer moral and spiritual guidance on such a broad range of issues and with such authority. The poor and disenfranchised in particular are in need of the Church's support. And most of those in greatest need are women. Women who need to understand that they are called not only to be mothers but should be educated, who are called to leadership positions and should have the capacity to control their reproductive choices, which will reduce their poverty.

One way to do this is to merely reduce the temperature on the abortion debate. In so doing, the Church can make a new start and end the divisive period the Church has endured. By considering abortion as one of many issues the Church cares about, the Church can recapture the moral leadership on the full range of issues on which its voice is so sorely needed, and so desperately lacking.

The Risen Christ first revealed Himself to a woman, Mary Magdalene, and the male Peter was upset. The story's significance may have been lost through the ages, but now as women awaken to the power that Christ gave us, we can claim our rightful leadership roles. It would be wonderful if the Church hierarchy would grasp this golden moment. But my instinct is that the changing attitude toward women that must occur will come as most reform and renewal movements do, from the ground up, from those who walk with the people, not those who dictate to them.

Once this happens, the Church will be able to regain the full scope of its social teaching and once again inspire Catholics and the world to care for the most vulnerable. This reformed Church can advance the vision of love of neighbor that the Gospels call for. As Jesus said, "As you did it to one of the least of these, you did it to me."

CHAPTER SEVEN

Moses Didn't Have a Bake Sale

T he rightward drift of both Catholic and Protestant churches during the past forty years has left an enormous number of Americans with the feeling that their church doesn't speak for them. But if we're honest, we can't pin all the blame on conservative clergy. The Religious Left has silenced itself. That part of the faith community that inspired the labor movement, marched against segregation, opposed the Vietnam War, and brought moral authority to America's efforts to fight poverty has all but disappeared from the national political discourse.

The results have been catastrophic. The values that used to animate the progressive movement—the notion that we share a responsibility to one another, that we

were, in fact, our brother's keepers—are steadily erod-
ing. One in every five American children starts his or
her life in poverty. Our grandparents are being driven
into bankruptcy because of prescription drug bills. And
corporate executives are pulling down salaries in the
tens if not hundreds of millions while cutting the health
benefits and pensions of their employees. And yet,
where is the righteous anger? Where are the calls to remember our responsibility to one another as children of
the same God? While religious leaders obsess about the
perceived sexual sins of others, where are our Ezekiels
to remind us that "this was the guilt of your sister
Sodom: She and her daughters were arrogant, overfed,
and unconcerned; they did not help the poor and
needy."

Sometime in the late 1960s and early 1970s, the Religious Left and the secular left got a divorce that weak-
ened both. Because the Religious Left has abstained
from the political debate, its moral vision cannot influence law and policy. And because progressive politicians seem reluctant to draw on the rich religious
tradition that shaped the history of our country, they
lack the moral weight to inspire our nation to reaffirm
its responsibilities.

Lately, a lot of polls have shown that Americans
don't know what Democrats stand for. They trust Democrats on the issues: the left routinely rates higher
among voters on important issues such as the economy,

education, health care, and retirement issues. But they fail to see a guiding philosophy. I think what the voters are saying is that they don't see a moral grounding to Democratic policies. It's not hard to see why. Today's Democrats tend to identify economics as the source of their policies, not the eternal values taught in the Scriptures. And it's hard to be inspired by economic theory.

How can we find our way back? The answer, I believe, is for religious progressives, clergy and laity alike, to return to the political sphere so that their words can have an impact on the shaping of our nation's future. There are examples to follow. Scattered throughout our country, there are people whose understanding of the Gospels has driven them to give of themselves and work for the betterment of their communities and their country. Their faith is at the very heart of their work. I hope that it can once again be the heart of our nation's greatness.

To be sure, there are risks for people of faith within the political arena. Power corrupts. And when faith chases after politics, faith itself can be corrupted. But in a democracy, the political system offers us the chance to express our belief in social justice on the national stage. A revived Religious Left, by emphasizing principles and values that form the beating heart of the Gospels, can extend the reach of justice and unite our country around the shared values of justice, mercy, and peacemaking. In this chapter, I hope to show how and why the Religious Left silenced itself, why we need its return, and whom we can turn to for inspiration.

When I think of the power of the Gospels to inspire social action, I think about Tony Campolo, the Baptist preacher and activist. I first heard him preach at the Renaissance Weekends in South Carolina and later at the Metropolitan AME Church in Washington before President Bill Clinton's Second Inaugural. Rev. Campolo is a faithful opponent of abortion on the grounds that all lives are sacred. But he is the first to admit that the faith community has become too narrow in their focus. "Evangelicals," he said in an interview with Beliefnet, "are so concerned with the unborn—as we should be—that we have failed to pay enough attention to the born."

When I spoke to him, he told me how he will often preach in conservative churches and start with the words, "I believe in the inerrancy of the Bible." People cheer and nod, happy that he is one of them—not those liberals who dismiss the miracles. "Then, I say 'which Bible? What about the Bible that says nations shall be judged on what they do for the least among us?'" He acknowledges that sometimes that tack is successful, sometimes not. People hear what they want.

Tony isn't just preaching the Word. He's living it. In 1965, he founded the Evangelical Association for the Promotion of Education, a group that sponsors and runs schools and youth activities throughout the world, from

Africa, to Haiti, to the slums of Philadelphia. In Haiti, he's worked with church leaders, evangelical or not, to create literacy centers. In Camden, New Jersey, Tony has started Urban Promise, a group that goes into some of the toughest neighborhoods in the country and offers them hope through tutoring and entrepreneurship programs. Perhaps most promisingly, Tony founded the Campolo School of Social Change. The school teaches Christians the tools they need to transform urban communities. Through his preaching, his advocacy, and his organizing, Tony is training the next generation of Christian progressives and setting them on the challenges that Jesus called us to address.

Tony's great insight, the reason he has been so successful at harnessing the power of faith toward the goal of social progress, is that he sees the inextricable connection between Christian faith and good works. Jesus did not merely preach. He didn't merely try to convert those He met. He actively tried to help. He healed the sick. He brought food to the poor. He stood up to hypocrisy and injustice. He was fearless in speaking truth to power. And He challenged those religious and secular authorities who wanted to silence Him.

The essence of Christianity is to live a life imbued with the Spirit of God. By acting with Christian mercy and compassion, we transform our lives into something holy and sacred. You just can't do that in forty-five minutes on Sunday. The Gospels tell us that it is an empty faith that confines itself within the walls of a church. And we can't really have a true relationship with Jesus if we don't let His example guide us to the places, people, and problems that He would visit were He alive today. We are closest to God when we embody the spirit of service and love.

Can there be another interpretation to Matthew's description of the Second Coming? As Matthew writes (25: 34–40),

> Then the king will say to those at his right hand, "Come O blessed of my father, inherit the kingdom prepared for you from the foundation of the world; for I was hungry and you gave me food, I was thirsty and you gave me drink, I was a stranger and you welcomed me, I was naked and you clothed me, I was sick and you visited me, I was in prison and you came to me." Then the righteous will answer him, "Lord, when did we see thee hungry and feed thee, or thirsty and give thee drink? And when did we see thee a stranger and welcome thee, or naked and clothe thee? And when did we see thee sick or in prison and visit thee?" And the king will answer them, "Truly, I say to you, as you did it to one of the least of my brethren, you did it to me."

Liberals often cite that passage with a feeling of self-satisfaction, thinking that it is we, not those callous Republicans, who truly care about the poor. But looking back on the past thirty years or so, I can't see much to be proud of. The Religious Left has been all but silent while conservatives have redefined faith and values in their own image. The country has become more unfeeling toward those in need, and the people who claim to care most for them have done precious little to stop them.

How did this happen?

The progression of the civil rights movement, and later the women's movement, both drove wedges. In the latter half of the 1960s, the brutality inflicted on Freedom Riders and marchers began to take its toll and many began to lose faith in the principles of nonviolence. At the same time, black leaders were being elected to office, taking clergy's role as the most prominent leaders in the black community. In the 1960s, the civil rights movement was in the hands of religious leaders like Dr. King, Rev. Ralph Abernathy, and Rev. Andrew Young. Young symbolized the transition by entering politics, winning election to Congress in 1972. He was joined by other prominent politicians such as Barbara Jordan, Shirley Chisholm, and John Lewis. I certainly don't mean to suggest this was a bad thing. Far from it. But the spiritual aspirations of the civil rights movement seemed to get lost along the way, and overall, the civil rights movement began speaking less of justice and all its religious connotations, and more about the legalistic definition of rights.

The women's movement was problematic as well.

The radical fringes of the movement were extremely critical of religious institutions and religion in general. That alienated many religious progressives, even though they may have subscribed to the same goals as the women's movement. Many religious progressives, too, were honestly troubled about the focus on abortion rights. Turning to the Republican Party was for many unthinkable. But once preservation of *Roe v. Wade* became a central, unquestionable tenet of progressive politics, many people of faith began to feel politically homeless.

In a way, both the civil rights and women's movements were undergoing a similar change, one reflected throughout our country's politics. Identity politics—whether in service of civil rights or the women's movement—drove religion out of the progressive movement. The Christian spirit, at its best, reflects those beautiful words of St. Paul: "There is neither Jew nor Greek, there is neither slave nor free, there is neither male nor female: for you are all one in Christ." If you substitute "in America" for "in Christ" you've described the best of the progressive movement as well. That's why they reinforced each other for so long. But liberal politics in the 1970s began saying just the opposite. The essence of politics became the difference between male and female, black and white, liberal and conservative, Northern and Southern. It's hard to maintain a feeling of brotherhood when you're constantly being reminded of our physical differences and told to ignore our shared spiritual nature.

The imbalance was never so evident as in the mid-1990s. Just after the Republicans took control of Congress, the Christian Coalition sent a letter to members of Congress asking for their support for both a tax cut for wealthy families and the Republican version of welfare reform, which denied aid for child care, health care, and job training. Glenn Poshard, a Democratic congressman from Illinois and a faithful Baptist, went to the floor of the House of Representatives and gave one of the most eloquent speeches I've ever read about how Christian faith should inform national politics.

> With all due respect to the Christian Coalition, where does it say in the Scriptures that the character of God is to give more to those who have and less to those who have not? . . . It should not be the position of the Christian community to slow down the growth of assistance to the poor while increasing the growth of assistance to the wealthy. . . . If there is one thing evident in the Scriptures, it is that God gives priority to the poor. . . . The least, the poorest, those who are at the bottom-most rung of the ladder—these are the ones to whom God gives the priority. This to me is the Christian message as I understand the Scriptures.

Poshard gave one of the clearest and most powerful calls for Christian activism in recent memory. But no one answered. There wasn't a single instance of anyone on the Christian Left coming to his defense or seconding his understanding of the relevance of the Gospel's teaching in the day's political debate. Nor did his colleagues tap into their own belief to counter the Christian Coalition. Poshard was just a lonely voice in the wilderness. The Christian Coalition, angered by Poshard's direct challenge to them, went on to target him for defeat (though unsuccessfully). And the politics of Washington just went along as always.

Religious progressives just can't afford to sit on the sidelines anymore while others use the name of God as a wedge against those with whom they disagree. It's time to follow our faith and let it guide our words and deeds not only inside our churches but in the larger world as well. The challenges our country faces today are challenges of the spirit. They are challenges of the soul. At their root, the problems come down to whether or not individuals feel as though their lives have intrinsic value and meaning; whether or not they are part of something larger than themselves that can serve as a source of courage and strength during tough times.

One of my inspirations is the example of Ruby Bridges, the six-year-old girl who initiated school desegregation in New Orleans in 1960. Day after day, this small girl walked past a gauntlet of angry, resentful adults shouting ugly threats and spitting curses at her. And yet each day, she would turn to these hateful people and smile. When Ruby was asked how she could bear such hatred, she explained:

> The minister came to our house and he said . . . not to worry, and I don't. The minister said God is watching and He won't forget because He never does. The minister says if I forgive the people, and smile at them and pray for them, God will keep a good eye on everything and He'll be our protection.

Ruby's innocence may be beyond our grasp, but her faith is not.

Consider the example of Allan Tibbels. Allan is a Lutheran minister who, until twenty years ago, ran a church in Howard County, Maryland, a wealthy suburban community between Washington and Baltimore. In 1981, while playing a rough game of basketball, Allan was hit by another player and was paralyzed from the neck down. He has spent the past twenty-five years in a wheelchair. Allan had always been interested in tackling the challenges of the inner city, but his accident, he says, gave him a renewed sense of urgency. In 1986, he and his wife, Susan, moved to one of the toughest neighborhoods in Baltimore, Sandtown. "Why go?" he reflects. "As Christians we are called to a place of hurt.

Christians feel blessed and our purpose is to extend yourself on behalf of the hurting world."

Demonstrating his boundless, indeed saintlike, faith, Allan believes the injury turned into a blessing. "God uses the context. When we moved into Sandtown, people thought that we were on welfare since I was in a wheelchair and that we could not afford to live anyplace else." This broke down barriers and opened people up to Him.

When they moved into the seventy-two-square-block neighborhood, there were one thousand families, with the average family income of $8,500 a year. Many of the houses were vacant. At that time there was not much happening in Sandtown. They recruited volunteers to clean up the trash but, says Tibbels, "we were more interested in dealing with the root problem—not symptoms. Not just cleaning up the trash, but education and home ownership. . . . Evangelism can't be just verbiage. You must truly love your neighbor. You must build a house." And build they did. Allan became the executive director of Habitat for Humanity, building homes for people in the neighborhood.

But Allan also recognized the limits to private charity. A couple of years later, the developer James Rouse came up with an idea to leverage federal money to help redevelop distressed communities. Rouse worked with local politicians to pass legislation authorizing loans to low-income families to buy homes. They called it the

Nehemiah Project, after the prophet who rebuilt the city of Jerusalem.

Rev. Tibbels's example shows two things: First, that each of us has the power to make a difference. Second, that local and national solutions to our biggest problems will come from a renewed understanding that we are bound to one another, not merely by geography or citizenship, but by spirit. We are all children of the same God. Once we start acting like it, there will be no challenge beyond our reach.

The key point that religious progressives need to understand is that working through politics, while difficult, greatly enhances our ability to do good. It's nice to deliver meals to the elderly, or mentor children. But has our nation ever done more to honor our fathers and mothers than when we created Social Security? Roosevelt understood that the New Deal represented something larger than creating government programs. "We call what we have been doing 'human security' and 'social justice.' In the last analysis," he once said, "all of those terms can be described by one word; and that is 'Christianity.'" And there can be no doubt as to the effect. The elderly used to be the poorest age group in our country. Today they are the wealthiest. That's a direct result of progressives working through the political system. Can we not, in the same spirit, with the same passion, work today to fulfill the commandment that we love our neighbors?

Few people understand and embody this spirit better than Rev. David Beckmann. Rev. Beckmann runs Bread for the World, a group representing 2,500 different Catholic, mainline Protestant, evangelical, and African-American churches that works to end hunger around the world and improve the lives of the world's poor. But unlike a lot of churches, they don't see a soup kitchen or food pantry as the end of their work, but the beginning. "If Christians want to help poor people around the world you've got to use two legs: the leg of charity and the leg of justice. If you use just one, you are hopping all the time." Rev. Beckmann cites the story of Moses as his inspiration. "God did not send Moses to Pharaoh to take up a collection for canned goods," he says. "He went with a political message to let the slaves go free."

He has a mighty mountain to overcome. Rev. Beckmann says that his experience is that nearly every congregant gives to food pantries, but only between 2 percent and 5 percent write to Congress. He refers to a 1996 Pew poll that found that 90 percent of ministers talk about poverty but don't consider it a primary religious issue. When presented with a list of questions as to what are religious issues, the ministers say the top two are the death penalty and abortion; poverty is tenth. "What do the ministers actually talk about?" he asks incredulously. "These preachers aren't talking about justice—they are just talking about charity."

Each year, Bread for the World members send a quarter-million letters to congressmen and other elected officials. More important, they form the grass roots of the organization's campaigns to influence policy. They've been terrifically successful. In the past ten years, their support has been critical to increasing funding to help African AIDS patients, alleviate the debt of Third World nations, and increase federal funding for food stamp programs.

Beckmann says that the work begins in changing the way ministers view the power they have to inspire and enlighten their congregants. "We want our hunger issues to be raised at worship," he explains. "Get people to [send] a letter one week, and next week put it in the collection basket, so it's not just bread and wine that we are offering to God. We want the whole church to get the idea that active citizenship for justice is part of our stewardship life. It is a fit offering to God. . . . St. Paul used his Roman citizenship to help the church grow. If St. Paul can use his Roman citizenship on behalf of Jesus, surely we who live in a democracy in the richest country in the world should use our citizenship to do God's work."

Churches can provide not only the spiritual framework for a new progressive movement but the infrastructure as well.

Thirty years ago, for instance, a group of activists from the legendary radical Saul Alinsky's Industrial

Areas Foundation started an organization called Baltimoreans United in Leadership Development, or BUILD. They soon found that while they were able to recruit volunteers for discrete projects, such as building a playground or stopping a highway from being built through a neighborhood, when the project was over, the group fell apart. BUILD wanted to create a consciousness of power that would bind people together for the fights, for the victories—and for the next fight. The organizers then figured that if they worked with preexisting organizations, one big step in the process would be addressed: They would not have to begin anew with each different fight.

Having decided to work through institutions, they were inevitably drawn to the most prominent and stable institutions in the inner city—churches. Currently, 95 percent of BUILD's affiliated institutions are churches. And during the past thirty years, they've become one of the most successful and stable organizations working to improve Baltimore neighborhoods. Not only have they lobbied the State General Assembly for funds to build playgrounds and redevelop abandoned areas, they've played decisive roles in the efforts to increase funding for children's health care and keeping predatory lenders out of urban neighborhoods.

Getting money for playgrounds may seem like small potatoes. But BUILD and organizations like them are laying a foundation. With simple, small steps forward, they're proving to religious people that the political system can help them do God's work. Will keeping predatory lenders out of the inner city change the world? Probably not. But every time a person of faith, or a congregation, or a group of churches enacts their vision of a more just and compassionate world, they help build the foundation for a renewal of the role of faith in the progressive movement and the leadership of our nation.

There can be no doubt that such a renewal is necessary. The ties that bind us as a nation and a people are coming undone. A young boy in inner-city Baltimore or out in the hill country of West Virginia feels that there is nothing at the end of the road for him. These young people watch as the rest of us go from peak to new peak of comfort, new cars, new computers, new homes built farther and farther from their own. Each day the dream gets further from their reach. And each day their hope for a better life and their faith that they live in a just nation diminishes.

Even those of us who live in comfort and security have a stake in this. This is a test of our spirit. Jesus taught us that to serve others is to be close to God. We can't get there just by singing in church or sitting at home reading self-help books. It isn't enough to toss some change into a collection plate.

When we deny our obligation to come to the aid of our brothers and sisters, we pass up an opportunity to move closer to God. The creation of a just and merciful society enriches all of us. First, because we are fulfilling our potential as individuals endowed by God with both reason and love. And second because we are making the most of our potential as a nation, which has been blessed by God with the prosperity to meet all the needs of all our people.

Conservatives often say that America is a "Christian nation." Liberals find this exclusionary, and I agree that when it's used it's often said to set Christians above those of other faiths. As offensive as this suggestion is, the primary sentiment I feel when I hear the phrase "Christian nation" isn't anger, but sadness. Wouldn't it be wonderful if we were, in fact, a truly Christian nation? Wouldn't it be wonderful if our laws and policies reflected Christ's compassion and concern for the poorest and most vulnerable among us? Wouldn't it be wonderful if our citizens showed the same love for one another that Christ held in His heart for all humankind? This may seem utopian. What troubles me isn't so much that we fall short. It's that most, including most who call themselves Christian, do not even seem to want to try.

I have hope that we can change this. While many on the Christian Right seem to have hardened their hearts to the needs of the poor and underprivileged, there is a large constituency among evangelicals, mainline Protestants, and Catholics alike who are eager to think hard about how they can live their faith.

I was inspired by a trip I took not long ago to meet with the mega-preacher and bestselling author Rick Warren. What he said truly astounded me. His story showed me how the same Bible can be so differently understood.

Warren founded the Saddleback Church in Lake Forest, California, in 1980. Since then his book *The Purpose-Driven Life* has sold some 25 million copies. He's trained a quarter of a million ministers through his seminars and Internet classes. His may be the largest church in the Southern Baptist Convention—he claims 16,000 in attendance each weekend and 50,000 names on the church roll, and he says it's the fastest-growing Baptist church in history.

When you meet Rick, he's warm and engaging. He does not put on airs. He's friendly and open, and impressed me with his sincerity. He wants to help. He wants to do the right thing. His philosophy, as *TIME* magazine summed it up, is simple—that God has a purpose for us: "to bring enjoyment to Him, to be a part of His family, to behave like Him, to serve Him and to act as His missionary. The payoff for abiding by these precepts, Warren promises, is reduced stress, sharper focus, simplified decision making, greater meaning to life and better preparation for eternity."

In other words, it's about one's own private happiness. After an hour or so of talking about Rick's ideas, I asked him where in his teachings he talked about helping *other* people, specifically the poor. Rick turned to me and said, with all honesty, that for the twenty-five years of his ministry, he had never, until recently, considered religion's role in helping the poor at all.

I was stunned. Yes, Rick had been reading the Bible, but he hadn't been reading *my* Bible.

His story, however, doesn't stop there. Recently, Rick has experienced something of a transformation. It began with his wife, Kay, who was reading an article about AIDS in Africa. The text she could handle, but the photos were too horrifying to her, and she put her hand over them in disgust. Then she forced herself to look, and saw pictures of some of the millions of children dying of AIDS. She told Rick about her revelation: that she had always thought AIDS was God's way of punishing the unworthy, but how could that be the case if so many children, innocent of any sin, could be afflicted?

At first, Rick wasn't impressed. What does that have to do with our work? he asked her. But Kay wouldn't be swayed and she insisted Rick see up close those who needed his help.

It was a life-changing experience, and it led Rick on a journey to reevaluate the foundations of his belief. Today, Warren told me, he reverse-tithes, giving away 90 percent of his money and keeping 10 percent for himself. He has developed a poverty plan, called his P.E.A.C.E. plan, which he first laid out in November

2003. It's an amazing document, acknowledging that for the first two decades his ministry really hadn't spread beyond helping his church, its members, and then other churches as well. It's a five-point plan focusing on improving the world, both spiritually and economically. "More than half of the world—that's three billion people—live on less than two dollars a day," he says. "One-sixth of the world's population lives in slums. Those are heart-breaking statistics. Proverbs 29:7 (NIV) says, *'The righteous care about justice for the poor, but the wicked have no such concern.'*" He told me that for his failure to recognize these needs earlier in his career, "I must repent." And that's not a casual word from a religious man.

Rick's transformation inspires me: If this powerful conservative evangelical pastor can see the light of the Social Gospel, there is hope that it can once again inspire our nation.

That's why it's so important that progressive people of faith return to the public sphere.

Rarely in our history has our nation been so polarized and divided. Red state from blue state. Republican from Democrat. Catholic from Protestant. Mainline from evangelical. The information age has only speeded up this disintegration of national identity. It's easier than ever before to go through life surrounding ourselves with people just like us, hearing ideas and information that serve only to confirm our own particular world-view. This may feel comforting to some. But it is poison to our country.

But for all that divides us, this we have in common: We are commanded to love our neighbor. Not in the abstract. Not merely in words. But with action.

As we share a common obligation, so, too, can we, in the fulfillment of that obligation, share a common future. We have the ability to raise our country up and ensure that it does live up to that potential. But it can't be done from the sidelines. If religious progressives reengage in politics, we can make the most of the gifts God has given our country. We can help the people who need it most. And we can give life to that part of our souls that knows that the path to holiness is one of service, sacrifice, and love.

This is how we can, as individuals and as a nation, meet the challenge that the prophet Micah set forth: to do justice, love mercy, and walk with the Lord.

CHAPTER EIGHT

Write the Vision on the Tablets

If Jesus were to walk among us again today, in the early years of the twenty-first century, witnessing the state of America's families, our culture, our politics, and our religious institutions, what would Jesus do?

We need not guess if we but consider what He did in the country of his birth twenty-one centuries ago. We who are Christians believe He died for our sins so that we may live, and that is central to our understanding of His role in our lives and in history. But before He died and rose again, He did walk among those who lived in that day, witnessing the state of families, the culture, politics, and religious institutions of ancient, Roman-occupied Israel.

And what *did* Jesus do?

He taught us to love one another. He told us to forgive each other, seventy times seven times. He said that whatever we do for the least of our brethren, we do for Him.

He did not shun the tax collector. He did not condemn the prostitute. In fact, He befriended outcasts. He helped each of them out of love; His only admonishments to them were to "sin no more."

The people who did face the scorn of Jesus, in fact, were the religious leaders, the powerful of society, the materialists who desecrated the Temple. He revealed the hypocrisy of those at the top and told the rich to sell what they had to help the poor.

Were Jesus to walk among us again today, I believe He would do the very same things. He would comfort the drug addicts, the homeless, people living with disease, children living unhealthy or unsafe lives. And He would challenge all of us who failed to come to their aid in the course of our individual lives or in the formulation of our collective policies.

Those in great need, living at the margins of society—shunned or ignored by so many who live in comfort—would find great succor from this twenty-first-century Savior. And those with great advantages who fail to apply them to the common good would be exposed and denounced as harshly as those who faced Jesus' wrath so long ago.

His was not only a personal morality. His was,

fundamentally, a public and civic morality, even—yes—a political one. Not that He took up political causes overtly; yet, the fruit of His labor presented a serious political challenge to the governmental and religious authorities of His day—so much so that they killed Him because of it.

Throughout our proud history, many Americans have understood the meaning of Christ's life and works. We're lucky in that regard—because not every nation can comfortably connect faith and politics. The Muslim world has an uneasy history of theocracy. In many former communist states, persecution of religious minorities in the last century has left deep scars. In Europe, the struggle to balance church and state is in many ways far more difficult than here in America. England's thorny history of an official national church helped seed the birth of the United States of America; France's alliance of church and opulent nobility led to a bloody revolution, the reverberations of which extend to the primarily secular state of today.

Here in America, we are blessed with twin traditions: On the one hand, we proudly announce in our Declaration of Independence that our inalienable rights are God-given and enshrine in our Constitution freedom of worship for every American; on the other, we offer clear protections against religious persecution—with a strict prohibition against establishing religion. We both respect faith and restrict it. We embrace religious minorities as well as those who choose not to believe in God.

That climate has given rise to so many powerful political, moral, religious movements—movements that have nimbly traveled between the pulpit and the public sector: abolitionism, the labor movement, and the civil rights movement chief among them. Each fight for justice had its roots in Jesus' teachings, and each understood that while advocacy might be powered by faith, it could not and should not confine itself to the space defined by the chapel walls.

Today, our sense of Christian virtue is both more and less political than it has been throughout our history.

It's *more* political in that our churches tend to dwell upon a few politically contentious questions—abortion and homosexuality in particular—at the cost of other important issues. I wouldn't suggest that abortion be ignored—it's a critical moral issue for millions of Catholics, myself included. Nor would I belittle the concerns of many of my fellow Catholics regarding our increasingly crass and sexually explicit culture—or about what they perceive as threats to the sanctity of marriage by having the state officially sanction homosexual unions.

At the very same time, our churches have become far *less* political—by shrinking from the public sphere and redefining morality as a limited set of personal choices alone.

The point here is that religious leaders are subverting their authority on issues of public moral responsibility by focusing exclusively on issues of private moral behavior. Even as it turns up the volume on a subset of moral imperatives, it barely whispers about so many other concerns that any honest reading of the Bible would reveal as being central to Jesus' teachings.

These two "faith-based" movements, one sliding toward partisan politics and the other moving away from participatory politics, have cheapened our churches. They have diminished our civic life. And they have ultimately failed our spirit.

Today, we've essentially created a one-dimensional cross: one that looks up and down at the morality in each individual human life, which of course is important, but fails to look consistently across human lives at our collective and social responsibilities. The focus on sexual abstinence, for example, misses the point that we are not just called to avoid evil but to do good. We are called to love, not just refrain from premarital sex.

The famous letter the Reverend Martin Luther King Jr. wrote from that Birmingham jail in April 1963 expressed a seamless synthesis of faith and social justice that once seemed so natural and now, sadly, feels so foreign:

> One day the South will know that when these disinherited children of God sat down at lunch counters, they were in reality standing up for what is

best in the American dream and for the most sacred values in our Judeo-Christian heritage, thereby bringing our nation back to those great wells of democracy which were dug deep by the founding fathers in their formulation of the Constitution and the Declaration of Independence.

Reverend King did not *wear* a "WWJD" bracelet. As a man full of flaws and sin like all of us, he nonetheless kept trying to do what Jesus might do in a world trapped by segregation.

Now more than ever, we need our churches to recapture and reclaim their true heritage, to get back their conscience and reclaim their credibility—to become, at once, more political and less partisan.

That process will begin by rediscovering the true source of Jesus' power—what we might call His holy trinity of ideals: faith, hope, and love.

Faith gives us the ability to believe what might, in an increasingly rational world, be increasingly hard for some to accept: that an Intelligent Being beyond our understanding has created this world and me in it. I can't prove it as though it were a scientific proposition, but, as Emily Dickinson has said about heaven, "Yet certain am I of the spot / As if the Checks were given." Because I believe that there is a Creator, I trust that the world has a purpose, that there is a shaping mind. I know that there is something transcendent about my life, something that is holy and sacred, something that laws of physics, chemistry, biology cannot describe; and I know that the same holiness is in every human being. I am therefore not only curious about the world but eager to venture forth into it.

Hope gives us courage to face the terror, sadness, sickness, and evil in the world. Hope lifts us even where the most powerful pessimism tugs at our heels. With hope, we resist despair, the fear that we are helpless to change our fate or to make the world a more just place. With hope, we envision a better future for ourselves, our children, and our grandchildren—and for the children and grandchildren of those less fortunate. No longer immobilized, we can act.

Love of course is, as St. Paul said, the greatest virtue—the one that gives birth to all others. And it is therefore the virtue that we are most in need of today. For in a world that seems to build barriers every day, love is a bridge. It asks us to reach beyond ourselves—to see the face of God in people who may not look like us, think like us, pray like us, or act like us. Love asks us to listen. And so love makes it possible to sacrifice for the other, to think about their needs, their hopes and dreams.

It is the power of love that enables us to feel what it is like to walk in our neighbor's shoes and to know in our hearts that every human being is a fellow child of God.

It is time for a spiritual rebirth in America. That

might surprise you to hear—because we're a very religious country. The media reminds us of that fact all the time. But no—it is time for a rebirth that recaptures the true creed of Jesus.

I believe too many mainline Protestant churches have drifted away from our basic spiritual needs. At the same time, after a glorious age of engagement around the civil rights movement, they have shied away from too much civic engagement.

For their part, the increasingly popular evangelical churches seem built on a foundation of self-improvement— appearing to make an almost explicit decision not to talk about our common responsibility to care for the poor, heal the sick, and build a world that's more just for every one of God's children. I don't mean to belittle the notion of self-improvement or equate it with selfishness: a nation with 100 million more people who are more responsible, loving, and caring would make us a far better nation. Those who attend evangelical churches no doubt also give to charity.

But just as Jesus' commandments resound far beyond the walls of the church, their effect on our soul resounds far beyond our own bodies and our own lives.

And as Rick Warren acknowledged in referring to himself, but aptly describing the tendency of many evangelicals, he just missed all those biblical passages that call on us to fight for justice, to care about the poor, the sick, the stranger.

And what about the Catholic Church? I have been saddened by the leadership's tendency to dwell on things like abortion, homosexuality, and premarital sex—to the diminishment or exclusion of so many other critical teachings. I have been outraged by the Church's defensive reaction to the molestation scandal. And I have been disappointed by an institution that seems to reflexively view any attempt to reform with suspicion—rather than considering the possibility that some change might bring the Church *closer* to God's true will.

If our churches can begin to be guided again by the compass of the cross—which points to faith, hope, and love—they will begin to walk down a new path of purpose.

Reformed and reborn churches will think of Christianity's role in the world expansively, as a fierce, independent, and uncompromising force for love—not as the purveyor of narrow personal prayer books and, all too often, partisan playbooks.

For the Catholic Church, that means beginning to preach a more balanced vision of the earthly ethics our faith requires—a bold, broad form of Christian virtue. It means having some humility and listening to the laity's view on the choice of bishops, priests, the role of women. It is difficult for bureaucracies to change, but the alternative is having millions of good, faithful people turn away. And it means amplifying the voices of leaders who understand the moral authority of the Church expansively, not narrowly. We should remember that St. Peter was quickly joined by St. Paul in the early days of the Church, with St. Paul being the primary proponent of reaching out to the world of the Gentiles, rather than focusing solely on the conversion of the Jewish people. And we should also remember that in choosing St. Peter and St. Paul as leaders of the Church, God chose two men who were themselves very flawed human beings. St. Peter, don't forget, denied Christ three times on the evening of His arrest. And St. Paul, prior to his conversion, actually persecuted Christians with a vengeance.

We don't have to conjure up such leaders as though we are writing a Hollywood script. They are in our recent past—think of the Catholic leaders who have practiced what they have preached: Dorothy Day, Daniel and Philip Berrigan, César Chávez, among many others who suffered for their public expressions of faith.

And they are in our midst today.

I think of Sister Helen Prejean, whose correspondence with convicted murderer Patrick Sonnier set her on a crusade against the death penalty and led her to found Survive, an organization committed to counseling family members of the victims of violence. Sister Prejean demonstrates that it is possible to see a spark of divinity even in the eyes of a murderer, and she has devoted her life to help redeem those whom others condemn as beyond redemption.

Or Sister Jeannine Gramick, who took to heart the

Church's call to extend love and respect to those who were outcast and founded a ministry for gay and lesbian Catholics. Despite the Vatican's condemnation of her work and its direct order to shut down her ministry, Sister Gramick feels a sacred obligation to build bridges between the Church she loves and the people she believes are worthy of respect and love in the eyes of the Church. In her response to the Vatican's criticism of her ministry, she wrote,

> The project of building bridges is always a dangerous one because the effort to establish communication between alienated parties (the Church and many lesbian/gay Catholics) is apt to encounter misunderstanding from both sides. . . . I have been criticized frequently by gay and lesbian people precisely because I have not rejected the magisterial teaching on homogenital activity. Unfortunately, I find that I am also criticized by the Church, which I dearly love, on suspicion of disloyalty to that teaching. It is my intent to present the truth of the Church's teachings in its integrity in such a way that will enable lesbian and gay persons to live an authentically Christian life and to convey more effectively my loyalty to the Church in my future ministry to them.

These women, and many more who share their spirit, stand at the fringes of the Church. But through their expansive vision of compassion and justice, they are widening the reach of God's love and bringing more people closer to God. But it is regrettably on the fringes of the Church—not part of its hierarchy.

And it is not only Catholicism that has a strong tradition of connecting public virtue with personal salvation. The Protestant tradition has an equally strong tradition of understanding social justice broadly—and of fighting, without apology or compromise, poverty, exploitation, and discrimination.

If we do not hear their stories, it is because they are focusing on local issues, rather than the divisive national issues that garner headlines. One of the best examples comes from my hometown of Baltimore: Rev. Frank Reed, who is the pastor of Bethel AME Church, which is home to 16,000 members. Not unlike many urban churches, about 20 percent of Rev. Reed's congregation is comprised of former addicts, and his church has established ministries to reach out to people struggling with addiction and to those in prison. When I spoke to him recently, he said that he felt a responsibility to "awaken people to their political responsibility, to the political nature of life." The Bible, he says, teaches us that we must be engaged in the effort to "meet the needs of the people. We must be involved politically."

And political involvement must extend beyond the borders of our community. God's Word is universal.

Our work to enact it must be as well. Few understand this as well as the author and activist Ronald Sider, who founded Evangelicals for Social Action thirty years ago. Sider has criticized mainline Protestant denominations for their neglect of evangelizing. But at the same time, he has been unyielding in his denunciations of evangelical congregations for ignoring economic injustice and hunger. The twin missions of evangelizing and social justice should work together. Speaking to a reporter for *Christianity Today*, Sider told the story of a young South African who, he said, "was literally afraid that if he became a Christian he would lose his passion for justice." The lack of social action, he says, is in fact an impediment to evangelism.

The mainline Protestant churches can recapture their power and relevance by answering the deep spiritual needs of their congregations. And the more evangelical churches who have focused almost solely on personal morality can begin expanding their writ to include concern for the common good.

Suppose you agree with my vision. How do we get there?

What if they continue to resist the call for change—the Catholic hierarchy continuing to underplay too many of Jesus' teachings, and too many Protestant churches preaching a very private form of virtue?

Then, the power is in the hands of individual

worshippers—who can and should try to reform their congregations and the larger institutions.

Some resist the call to reform the churches from within. Yes, they may attend services and contribute to the collection plate, but they are not spiritually engaged. They lack the guidance of a moral authority and the rich, caring life that comes from community. Others simply abandon their churches, staying at home on Sundays. In politics, we call this "voting with your feet." Sometimes it happens through affirmative choice, sometimes it is just apathy. But for those who believe in Jesus, abandoning the churches will not help to shape a religious institution that is true to the teachings of the Gospels that is needed by so many of us.

I urge those feeling disillusioned not only to keep going to church but to get involved. Meet with your priest or minister. Try to organize the congregation to do things that benefit the community.

If you speak, others of like mind will not only listen. Their voices will join the chorus, too. And this choir can, over the long run, be far more important than the one that sings the psalms.

These "movements" tend to begin locally, but when they are strong and heartfelt, there is no limit to what they can accomplish.

It is probably easier to reform and renew Protestant congregations than the Catholic Church, for they have a long tradition of bottom-up reform. But those who are committed to change in the Catholic Church, too, have happily carved out a path for themselves and our Church.

In the mid-1970s a group of dissident Catholics grew impatient with the Church's resistance to the voices of the laity and founded Call to Action. The group's goal, according to founders Dan and Sheila Daley, is "to accept our responsibility to reinvent the Church from the ground up modeled on an American charism; the spirit of open consultation, the new way of being Church in America." The group organizes local faith communities that can develop their own liturgies in the hope that their egalitarian spirit and worship will filter up through the hierarchy of the Church. While I don't agree with some of the iterations these local communities take, the effort to open up the Church to new voices could be invaluably revitalizing.

In the wake of the Church's pederasty scandals, several new efforts to reform the Church sprang up and have grown into forces that have the power to open up the Church to the voices of the laity. Geoffrey Boisi, a former vice chair of investment at JP Morgan Chase & Company, pulled together a group of business leaders, clergy, and intellectuals to increase lay involvement in the financial activities of the Church called The Church in the Twenty-First Century. Hoping to bring business principles of accountability and transparency to the Church hierarchy, Boisi intends to bring sunlight to the secretive decision-making that allowed bishops around the country to hide the intances of sexual abuse, allowing for more children to be victimized.

More prominently, the organization Voice of the Faithful has used the scandals as a way of mobilizing efforts to reform the "pay, pray, and obey" attitude of the Church hierarchy. Voice of the Faithful has come to the aid of the victims of abuse, spoken up on behalf of those priests who have fulfilled their calling with integrity and compassion, and fought to open up Church governance to the laity.

These efforts at reform have begun to have an effect and have made parishes more responsive to their congregations. And there is much more we can do.

If we call on the Church's leadership to reform from within and it refuses to budge, we can form Eucharistic communities that keep alive the idea that women can be priests, that men might someday be allowed to remain priests when they are married.

And we can call on the Church to be more transparent about how its money is spent. In the modern world, an institution's financial decisions are its moral decisions. All Catholics are shareholders in our Church and should begin acting that way.

In fact, when I once asked Theodore Edgar Cardinal McCarrick why he did not lead a reform movement in the Church, he demurred, saying that reform movements don't come from the hierarchy, but from the bottom up. That of course has been true in Catholic history—the Franciscans, Dominicans, Jesuits, all grew as a way to purify the Church.

The burden is on us. The unfortunate reality is that those of us who wait for the hierarchy could find ourselves waiting forever.

The process of reform is different in mainline Protestant and evangelical churches, but the principles are no different. When progressive members of the congregation believe that their faith is in some way being shortchanged, it is their duty and opportunity to lead the faithful somewhere better.

The churches I envision will not hesitate to chastise those who neglect the poor and ignore the sick. Their clergy will be righteously angered by inequality and by unjust war. They will not forget to remind Jesus' followers that we are "the salt of the earth," responsible for preserving God's good earth. They will spurn shallow consumerism. They will be more troubled by the torture of prisoners than by same-sex marriage.

Perhaps most important, the reborn churches of the twenty-first century will care as much about the actions of groups of people and governments as they will about personal moral behavior. While it's true that people make the world, the world also makes people. And it's time our most powerful moral authorities made clear that the need to better society comes before self-fulfillment and self-improvement, not the other way around. The Christian self comes with loving one another and not simply from improving oneself. Indeed, we cannot have a purposeful life that is pleasing to God without leading a life devoted to our fellow human beings.

I am encouraged by Pope Benedict XVI's first encyclical, *Deus Caritas Est*, which was both a warmhearted disquisition on love and a ringing call to *service* to the least among us. He wrote, "love for widows and orphans, prisoners, and the sick and needy of every kind, is as essential to [the Church] as the ministry of the sacraments and preaching of the Gospel.... For the Church, charity is not a kind of welfare activity which could equally well be left to others, but is a part of her nature, an indispensable expression of her very being."

The stakes are high. If the Church refuses to reform or simply obeys the law of inertia and stays stuck in its ways, many of us will continue to meet in smaller Eucharistic communities, or in interfaith groups, to satisfy this yearning. If radio stations stop playing music, you can be sure that the people will find it elsewhere.

And the consequences of reinvigorated Christian churches reach far beyond our houses of worship. If our churches are true to their creed, our civic life, too, can be reborn.

When the churches rediscover their true moral center by recalling the full teachings of Jesus, that can help spur a spiritually based political revival throughout America. It can help *reverse* the growing polarization between the parties by making clear that neither has a monopoly on God and neither is today sufficiently guided by faith, hope, and love.

Those who sit on either side of the aisle in Congress have something in common with those who pray in pews throughout America: They are human souls with original sin and the capacity to do so much good for our communities, our nation, and our world.

But today those better instincts, that higher calling, is being hamstrung by churches that too narrowly understand their mission and too cynically align themselves with politicians.

I believe that if our churches were consistently preaching and teaching and focusing our attention on public morality as well as private actions, our politics—on both sides of the aisle—would be more focused on justice, on attention to the poor, and on preservation of the earth, among other things.

It turns out following the commandments of our God and learning to lead politically aren't very different from each another.

A growing chorus of scientists tells us that human activity is making the earth warmer; even without knowing precisely what the damage might be, such a dramatic environmental shift is disturbing. Christian virtue would take bold steps to protect and preserve God's creation, even if it means putting restrictions on the businesses that appear to be driving the change.

A billion of the world's people live on less than a

dollar a day, and 36 million Americans live in poverty. Do we accept the economy in which we live as a given or let our love for our fellow man guide us to devise new ways to help those in need by extending access to affordable housing, job training, and higher education? Can't we be just to the stranger—to the immigrant who wants only what our ancestors also yearned for, a chance to make a better life for themselves and their families?

And more than 40 million Americans—and growing—have no health insurance. They don't get regular check-ups. Problems simple to treat in their early stages can become fatal if left to fester. Who is making the clear moral case that, consistent with the foundations of our faith, that is wrong?

We are called to work for justice—and to express rage at injustice. Over and over again, our religious traditions say that the worst injustices are committed by those who care more for money (and power and fame and other material signs of "success") than for each other.

And if you find yourself recoiling at this language, thinking it all sounds too trite and partisan, ask yourself why. Why has the language of justice lost its power? Why have we let it be displaced by partisan rhetoric? Jesus didn't use talking points.

Have we become so weary and cynical that the second a moral problem begins to sound "tainted" by politics, we tune it out, for fear of getting trapped in a cycle of political recrimination?

We can do better. In a world with more complex problems and more power to solve them than ever before, we must do better.

Neither you nor I nor the family down the street can afford to wait passively for our churches to change or for the hierarchy to take its political responsibilities. With love in our hearts, care in our conversations, and understanding in our minds, we all can renew the churches. It is up to us who hunger and search for justice to help our churches fulfill their rightful mission.

We can begin to rediscover the deeper meaning and answer the deeper calling of our faith, whether or not our churches and our political parties change course. And that, in turn, can bring about change from the bottom up. Much of our political and religious rhetoric may be bankrupt. But we are not impotent. We can join with others to reinvigorate our commitment to the common good. Faith and justice are not only compatible; they are powerfully complementary.

Such a new Great Awakening would require us to change the way we lead our private and public lives. The Bible should remain an unparalleled source of inspiration and comfort, but not an object of idol worship or a buffer from the real world.

"A religious man is a person who holds God and man in one thought at one time, at all times, who suffers harm done to others, whose greatest passion is compassion, whose greatest strength is love and defiance of despair," wrote Rabbi Abraham Joshua Heschel. A *mitzvah*, he once said, is "a prayer in the form of a deed."

Once we take that first, fundamental risk and let the love of God and of each other fill our lives and our actions, it is like the experience of falling in love. We will find energy, enthusiasm, even joy in the experience of helping one another, even if the objects of our affection are people we don't know, may never meet, or might even fear if we met them on a deserted street corner. These are the spiritual roots of our work. They give us strength and inspiration to move forward.

God has given us this bountiful earth and it is our responsibility to nurture it and serve those who inhabit it. We care for our families and friends, we volunteer in our communities, we help our churches stay true to the Gospels, and we engage in the politics of justice. Jesus prayed that God's "will shall be done on earth." He understood that we must never give up trying.

Erik Kolbell writes in *What Jesus Meant*: "The point of Christianity is not simply to withstand life and abide suffering but to embrace life and redeem suffering. . . . In order to put flesh on the bones of a fragile faith, people will have to band together, look after one another, and bind to one another with a love that is greater than the sum total of all the jealousies and resentments that might now keep us apart."

This has been our challenge ever since we were ejected from the Garden of Eden, where all our needs were attended to, and we had no need for each other, save companionship. Because we need each other, we have a responsibility to make a contribution to one another, to love our neighbor, and to judge not, lest we be judged.

As my father said in that interview with David Frost nearly forty years ago, "You can always find someone that has a more difficult time than you do, has suffered more, and has faced some more difficult time one way or the other." You can always find someone; but too many of us, for far too long, have given up even looking.

For God's sake, if not our own, we must lift our gazes, individually and collectively, beyond ourselves. And in so doing, we will know that just as surely as history judges us, we will be able to judge ourselves. We have listened to our conscience.

In claiming that I understand we have a duty to care for the least among us, I may be accused of not living up to what He said myself. That I don't deny. I can't pretend that I am not sinful or weak. I am. Still, faith gives the enormous power of transformation. We can forgive, we can heal, and we can be healed and forgiven. The faith that has the power to move mountains can also tackle the seemingly impossible challenges—poverty, hunger, disease, violence. When powered by faith—given strength by Jesus—we can act. And those actions, and the hope that accompanies those actions, can be a source of enormous liberation. We need not be stuck in our anger, our bitterness, our frustration. Just the opposite. To believe means that we can be healed and enjoy an enormous sense of freedom.

Let us let the power of Matthew course through our veins: "You received without paying, give without paying."

This book was written with Christians in mind. But I hope its message is heard by all people of faith in America. It is time we stopped distorting faith to serve politics or silencing the better angels of our nature. It is time we started allowing faith to breathe freely and speak honestly, seeing the holy in our fellow human beings and our duty to one another on God's earth.

Come, Holy Ghost, fill the hearts of Your faithful and enkindle in them the fire of Your divine love. Send forth Your spirit and they shall be created and You shall renew the face of the earth.

BIBLIOGRAPHY

American Views on Religion, Politics and Public Policy, April 2001, The Pew Research Center, Washington, D.C.

Arendt, Hannah 1963, *On Revolution*, Viking, New York.

Bauer, G. L., & Dobson, Dr. J. 1990, *Children at Risk: The Battle for the Hearts and Minds of Our Kids*, Word Publishing, Dallas, London, Vancouver/Melbourne.

Bell, J. S., & Dawson, A. P. 2004, *From the Library of C. S. Lewis*, Waterbrook Press, Colorado.

Berger, Peter L. 1970, *A Rumor of Angels*, Anchor, Garden City, New York.

Blank, R. M., & McGurn, W. 2004, *Is the Market Moral? A Dialogue on Religion, Economics & Justice*, Brookings Institution Press, Washington, D.C.

Branch, Taylor 1988, *Parting the Waters*, Simon & Schuster, New York.

Caiazza, Amy 2005, *The Ties That Bind: Women's Public Vision for Politics, Religion and Civil Society*, Institute for Women's Policy Research, Washington, D.C.

Callahan, Daniel 1970, *Abortion: Law, Choice and Morality*, Macmillan, New York, Canada.

Chittister, Joan D. 1998, *Heart of Flesh: A Feminist Spirituality for Women and Men*, William B. Eerdmans, Michigan.

Chittister, Joan 1999, *In Search of Belief*, Liguori/Triumph, Missouri.

Chittister, Joan 2000, *The Friendship of Women: A Spiritual Tradition*, Benetvision, Erie, Pennsylvania.

Church, Forrest 1991, *God and Other Famous Liberals: Recapturing Bible, Flag and Family from the Far Right*, Walker, New York.

Church, Forrest 2002, *The American Creed*, St. Martin's/Griffin, New York.

Church, Forrest 2004, *Freedom from Fear*, St. Martin's, New York.

Church, Forrest 2004, *The Separation of Church and State*, Beacon Press, Boston.

Clark, Elizabeth 1983, *Women in the Early Church*, Michael Glazier, Wilmington, Delaware.

Cox, Harvey 1965, *The Secular City*, Macmillan, New York.

Dale, Graham 2000, *God's Politicians: The Christian Contribution to 100 Years of Labour*, HarperCollins, London.

Daly, Mary 1968, *The Church and the Second Sex*, Beacon Press, Boston.

Daly, Mary 1973, *Beyond God the Father*, Beacon Press, Boston.

D'Antonio, W. V., Davidson, J. D., Hoge, D. R., & Meyer, K. 2001, *American Catholics: Gender, Generation, and Commitment*, AltaMira Press, Lanham, Maryland.

Day, Dorothy 1953, *The Long Loneliness: An Autobiography*, Harper & Row, San Francisco.

Day, Dorothy 1960, *Thérèse*, Templegate, Springfield, Illinois.

DiIulio, J., Jr., & Dionne, E. J., Jr. 2000, *What's God to Do with the American Experiment*, Brookings Institution Press, Washington, D.C.

Dillenberger, John 1961, *Martin Luther: Selections from His Writings*, Doubleday, New York.

Dionne, E. J., Jr., & Chen Ming Hsu 2001, *Sacred Places, Civic Purposes*, Brookings Institution Press, Washington, D.C.

Ebest, R., & Ebest, S. B. 2003, *Reconciling Catholicism and Feminism?*, University of Notre Dame Press, Notre Dame, Indiana.

Eidsmoe, John 1987, *Christianity and the Constitution*, Baker Books, Grand Rapids, Michigan.

Elie, Paul 2003, *The Life You Save May Be Your Own: An*

American Pilgrimage, Farrar, Straus & Giroux, New York.

Fiorenza, Elisabeth Schüssler 1994, *In Memory of Her: A Feminist Theological Reconstruction of Christian Origins*, Crossroad, New York.

Frank, Thomas 2004, *What's the Matter with Kansas?*, Henry Holt, New York.

Goodwin, Doris Kearns 1987, *The Fitzgeralds and the Kennedys*, Simon & Schuster, New York.

Gornik, Mark R. 2002, *To Live in Peace: Biblical Faith and the Changing Inner City*, William B. Eerdmans, Grand Rapids, Michigan.

Guthman, E. O., & Allen, C. R. 1993, *RFK: Collected Speeches*, Viking, New York.

Hadden, Jeffrey 1969, *The Gathering Storm in the Churches*, Anchor, Garden City, New York.

Harrington, Michael 1983, *The Politics at God's Funeral*, Penguin, New York.

Harrison, Kathryn 2003, *Saint Thérèse of Lisieux*, Penguin, New York.

Henry, Carl F. H. 1947, *The Uneasy Conscience of Modern Fundamentalism*, William B. Eerdmans, Grand Rapids, Michigan.

Hilkert, Mary Catherine 2001, *Speaking with Authority*, Paulist Press, Mahwah, New Jersey.

Hoge, D. R., & Wenger, J. E. 2003, *Evolving Visions of the Priesthood*, Liturgical Press, Collegeville, Minnesota.

Huffington, Arianna 2004, *Fanatics and Fools*, Miramax Books, New York.

Hunt, John Gabriel 1995, *The Inaugural Addresses of the Presidents*, Random House, New York.

Jacoby, Susan 2004, *Freethinkers: A History of American Secularism*, Metropolitan Books, New York.

Jefferson, Thomas 1975, *Thomas Jefferson's Life of Jesus*, Templegate, Springfield, Illinois.

Jefferson, Thomas 1989, *The Jefferson Bible: The Life and Morals of Jesus of Nazareth*, Beacon Press, Boston.

Johnson, Elizabeth 2002, *The Church Women Want*, Crossroad, New York.

Kane, P., Kenneally, J., & Kennelly, K. 2001, *Gender Identities in American Catholicism*, Orbis, Maryknoll, New York.

Kengor, Paul 2004, *God and Ronald Reagan*, Regan-Books, New York.

Kidd, Sue Monk 1990, *When the Heart Waits*, Harper-SanFrancisco.

Kidd, Sue M. 1995, *The Dance of the Dissident Daughter*, HarperSanFrancisco.

Kolbell, Erik 2006, *What Jesus Meant*, Penguin, New York.

Krodel, G. A., Lazareth, W. H., Clarence, L. L., & Olson, O. 1976, *The Left Hand of God*, Fortress Press, Philadelphia.

LaCugna, Catherine Mowry 1993, *Freeing Theology: The*

Essentials of Theology in Feminist Perspective, Harper-SanFrancisco.

Lee, S. M., & Bernard, J. 2000, *The Catholic Experience of Small Christian Communities*, Paulist Press, New York, Mahwah, New Jersey.

Lewis, C. S. 1998, *C. S. Lewis on Faith*, Thomas Nelson, Tennessee.

Life in All Its Fullness: The Word of God and Human Rights, 1992, Baptist Joint Committee, Washington, D.C.

Macafee, Norman 2004, *The Gospel According to RFK*, Westview Press, Colorado.

Manning, Brennan 1999, *The Ragamuffin Gospel*, Multnomah, Sisters, Oregon.

Mansfield, Stephen 2003, *The Faith of George W. Bush*, Penguin, New York.

Marshall, P., & Manuel, D. 1977, *The Light and the Glory*, Fleming H. Revell, Grand Rapids, Michigan.

Martin, Celine 1997, *My Sister Saint Thérèse*, Tan Books and Publishers, Rockford, Illinois.

Martin, Marty 2004, *Martin Luther*, Penguin, New York.

Martin, William 1996, *With God on Our Side: The Rise of the Religious Right in America*, Broadway Books, New York.

Meninger, William A. 2000, *Bringing "The Imitation of Christ" into the 21st Century*, Continuum, New York.

Miller, Perry 1956, *Errand into the Wilderness*, Harper Torchbooks, New York.

Morgan, Edmund 1958, *The Puritan Dilemma*, Little, Brown, Boston, Toronto.

Mouw, Richard J. 1992, *Uncommon Decency: Christian Civility in an Uncivil World*, Intervarsity Press, Downer's Grove, Illinois.

A Nationwide Poll of Catholics on Issues Regarding the Catholic Church, 2003, Zogby International, Washington, D.C.

Niebuhr, H. Richard 1951, *Christ and Culture*, Harper & Row, New York, Evanston, Illinois.

Niebuhr, Reinhold 1932, *Moral Man and Immoral Society*, Charles Scribner's Sons, New York, London.

Niebuhr, Reinhold 1944, *The Children of Light and the Children of Darkness*, Charles Scribner's Sons, New York.

Niebuhr, Reinhold 1956, *An Interpretation of Christian Ethics*, Meridian Books, New York.

Niebuhr, Reinhold 1964, *The Nature and Destiny of Man*, Charles Scribner's Sons, New York.

Nouwen, Henry 1997, *Life of the Beloved*, Crossroad, New York.

Pagels, Elaine 1988, *Adam, Eve, and the Serpent*, Random House, New York.

Prothero, Stephen 2003, *American Jesus*, Farrar, Straus & Giroux, New York.

Rauschenbusch, Walter 1907, *Christianity and the Social Crisis*, Macmillan, New York.

Ryan, John Augustine 1906, *A Living Wage: Its Ethical and Economic Aspects*, Macmillan, New York.

Smith, Christian 2002, *Christian America? What Evangelicals Really Want*, University of California Press, Berkeley, Los Angeles, London.

Steinfels, Peter 2003, *A People Adrift*, Simon & Schuster, New York.

Wallis, Jim 1995, *The Soul of Politics: Beyond "Religious Right" and "Secular Left,"* New Press, New York.

Wallis, Jim 2005, *Faith Works: How to Live Your Beliefs and Ignite Positive Social Change*, Random House, New York.

Wallis, Jim 2005, *God's Politics: Why the Right Gets It Wrong and the Left Doesn't Get It*, HarperCollins, New York.

Wills, Garry 1990, *St. Augustine*, Penguin Lives, New York.

Wills, Garry 2002, *Why I Am a Catholic*, Mariner Books, New York.

Wills, Garry 2006, *What Jesus Meant*, Viking, New York.